An Introduction to
Catholic Social Teaching

Rodger Charles SJ

FAMILY PUBLICATIONS   OXFORD

IGNATIUS PRESS   SAN FRANCISCO

Cover design by Richard J S Brown

Cover photograph of Polish workers
occupying the Lenin shipyard in Gdansk,
Maciej Macierzynski, 1988
Corbis/Reuters

Published with ecclesiastical permission

Family Publications
77 Banbury Road, Oxford OX2 6LF UK
Tel: 01865 514408
ISBN 1–871217–30–X Paperback
ISBN 1–871217–31–8 Hardback

Ignatius Press
San Francisco USA
ISBN 0–89870–789–7

Library of Congress catalogue number 99–68464

Printed in England

To the memory of my sister Anne
who was all goodness and love

Contents

Chapter Two: Ethics and Political Society

Preface

The purpose of this book is to open up the social teaching of the Church to a wider audience. It is based on the last chapter of my *Christian Social Witness and Teaching: the Catholic Tradition from Genesis to Centesimus Annus*, published in two volumes by Gracewing in 1998. It extends and simplifies that chapter, making it more schematic and presenting key passages from the main social documents as illustrations. I have telescoped these passages from the original texts, taking only a phrase or sentence here and there so that the essential teaching stands out; I have added linking words where necessary in order to make the edited version read smoothly. The literary genre to which the social documents (especially encyclicals) belong does not encourage crispness and conciseness of language. I have added introductions to and commentaries on each section where needed, in order to weave the whole together.

'The social teaching of the Church' as a phrase usually refers to the modern corpus, but there is a social teaching in the Scriptures, and this teaching has developed within the Tradition of the Church; this evolution is examined in the first volume of *Christian Social Witness and Teaching*. Most of the modern corpus consists of social 'encyclicals' (circular letters) written by the popes since Leo XIII [1878–1903]. They are referred to by the first two or three words of the official (usually Latin) texts. Hence, for example, *Rerum Novarum* ('of new things', i.e. controversial changes in society caused by the industrial revolution), issued in 1891. Although there had been social encyclicals before, this one is justifiably seen as pivotal.

These documents are all basically moral and spiritual tracts or extended homilies. The Church has no competence in the technicalities of sociology, nor in political or economic theory and organisation: each has its own legitimate autonomy under reason and the natural law. Her competence is in giving guidance on the moral and spiritual consequences of the decisions and policies made in these spheres. She has the right to give us such guidance because these consequences affect the good of mankind, made in God's image and likeness. Since man must be free to choose his own eternal destiny, he must have political and economic freedom, and for this reason the Church is not politically partisan; her social teaching is not a party programme, though different parties will find similarities between her moral guidance and their policies. She has always had and always will have a preferential option for the poor, just like her master Jesus Christ, the poor being those who suffer hardship and injustice from whatever cause; they are, therefore, of all social classes, but mainly from those whose deprivation is social and economic. Such people are not to be seen as a proletariat, but as sons and daughters of God, all of whom must have access to a decent livelihood.

The social documents respond to specific situations and so depend on the reading of the signs of the times; but reading the signs of the times is not an exact science, and allows for different interpretations and revision in the light of further experience and knowledge. There will always be elements of the provisional in the Church's teaching in this area. However, the moral judgements involved concerning what is good and fitting for the dignity of the human being are not provisional, but binding on the conscience of all Catholics.

The main source in English for the social encyclicals is the last five volumes of Claudia Carlen's *Papal Pronouncements and Encyclicals 1740–1981* [Ann Arbor, Michigan 1991], which include them all. The social encyclicals of John Paul II may be found in *The Encyclicals of John Paul II* [J. H. Miller, Huntingdon, Indiana 1996]. *Proclaiming Justice and Peace* [M. Walsh and B. Davies, Mystic, Connecticut 1991] is a useful collection of fourteen modern documents, but it is by no means exhaustive. Volume 2 of my own *Christian Social Witness and Teaching* is more complete, containing detailed summaries of and key excerpts from the main modern corpus, some 34 documents in all, in their historical contexts. These are analysed under the subheadings of Ethics and Civil Society, Ethics and Political Society and Ethics and Economic Society. Certain sites on the internet now offer English versions of the vast majority of Vatican documents, including the social ones (see, for example, www.ewtn.com/ewtn/library/search.asp or the Vatican's site at www.vatican.va).

The following documents are the main ones referred to in the text, together with their sources:

Centesimus Annus, 1991, John Paul II	Miller
Diuturnum Illud, 1881, Leo XIII	Carlen
Divini Redemptoris, 1937, Pius X	Carlen
Evangelium Vitae, 1995, John Paul II	Miller
Familiaris Consortio, 1981, John Paul II	Miller
Gaudium et Spes, 1965, Second Vatican Council	A Flannery [ed], *Vatican Council II: Conciliar and Post-Conciliar Documents*, Wilmington, Delaware 1975
Humanae Vitae, 1968, Paul VI	Miller
Laborem Exercens, 1981, John Paul II	Miller
Libertatis Conscientia, 1986, CDF	A T Hennelly [ed], *Liberation Theology: a Documentary History*, New York 1990
Mater et Magistra, 1961, John XXIII	Walsh and Davies
Mit Brennender Sorge, 1937, Pius XI	Carlen
Octogesima Adveniens, 1971, Paul VI	Walsh and Davies
Pacem in Terris, 1963, John XXIII	Walsh and Davies
Populorum Progressio, 1967, Paul VI	Walsh and Davies
Quadragesimo Anno, 1931, Pius XI	Walsh and Davies
Redemptor Hominis, 1979, John Paul II	Miller
Rerum Novarum, 1891, Leo XIII	Walsh and Davies
Sollicitudo Rei Socialis, 1987, John Paul II	Miller
Summi Ponificatus, 1939, Pius XII	Carlen
Tertio Millennio Adveniente, 1994, John Paul II	Catholic Truth Society, London 1999
Veritatis Splendor, 1993, John Paul II	Miller

There are also quotations from addresses given by Pius XI, Pius XII and John Paul II, and texts from the *Summa Theologiae* and *De Regimine Principum* of St Thomas, and St Robert's *De Membris Ecclesiae*. The sources are given in the text.

R. Charles SJ
Campion Hall, Oxford   *Whit Sunday 1999*

Chapter One
Ethics and civil society

1. Introduction

'Society' can mean any association of persons who come together to achieve a common end, though the word usually refers to the whole complex of social organisation which constitutes *political society* – the 'state'. There are many theories about how society in this sense evolved. Logically thinking, it is necessary to posit a less formal association of citizens – *civil* or *civic society* – preceding it, and out of whose needs it grew. Within the state the organisation of economic life constitutes an entity of its own – *economic society*. All three – civic, political and economic societies – present their own ethical problems.

The scriptures tell us that human beings are made in God's image and likeness, in that they have free will and intelligence. They can then know the difference between right and wrong and can choose between them. They are morally responsible for their freely chosen acts and their human dignity lies in their ability to freely choose what is right. Any social organisation of which they are part must therefore respect this dignity. Man is the purpose and end of every society, and the State (and any social organisation) exists to serve him. He does not exist to serve them.

The family unit, based on lifelong monogamy, is the basis of society. Within family life individuals develop their personalities, under the guidance of their parents. As adults, they in their turn can lead free, independent and morally responsible lives, choosing to marry and found families if they wish, and co-operate with others in building up human society. This pre-political or civil society, which does not have the power to make and enforce laws, needs to be complemented by a political society which does have this power.

However, this is an assumption, a theory. In fact, it is into political society that most of us are born, and there are few examples of such a progression from a civil society to a political one. One might be seen, however, in the American West in the nineteenth century, where there were communities in the 'territories' before new states were formed. Federal law held sway there to some extent, and the citizens organised for basic cultural and economic purposes, and established social conventions accordingly; but it was not until a formal system of government, a political society, was set up in each territory that laws could be properly made and enforced over all the areas required by a civilised society. Another example might be seen in this century in Poland: before the final collapse of real socialism there in the late 1980s, the importance and viability of civil society was demonstrated. There the people gradually denied legitimacy to the state and set up their own informal associations which controlled much of civil life by agreement, only conceding to the law and government what was necessary for good order. Finally, the political system lost its legitimacy and authority, and civil society chose its own government once more. We can also see civil society as the basis of the political during the time of an election in a democracy. The old government is in power, but it does not choose the new one. In the act of casting its ballots, civil society momentarily reclaims its power from the government and transfers it to another.

Civil society, therefore, is a reality even though, in most cases, political society is in place at the time of our birth and we always have been subject to it. The knowledge that this society is real gives us an insight into the nature of human rights, rights which the State did not give us and cannot take away from us, and also into what responsibilities we owe the State, to whose authority we submit ourselves because of our need of its services. It also makes us aware that, if the political regime becomes oppressive, we have a right to oppose it, because it exists for the purpose of serving civil society. For this reason, in the last analysis, and with many qualifications, there is a right to revolt against a seriously unjust government.

2. The human person is the end and purpose of every social organisation

Human experience has shown that, while human social organisation in civil and political society is, in principle, beneficial and necessary, the latter especially can be oppressive. Those who control the state can do so for their own purposes and not for the purposes of the *common good* – the good of the whole people, and of each person, under just law – which is the whole purpose of political society. The first principle of all social organisation is, therefore, that it must serve the human person, made in God's image and likeness. The human person is possessed of rights of which he must not be deprived and corresponding human duties which he must not neglect.

The second principle is that human beings are by nature social, and that they need to live in an organised society with others so that they can develop socially, intellectually, economically and spiritually. Though they can live in isolation if circumstances give them no choice, or if they have the temperament for it and freely choose it, social living is necessary for normal human development. Humans have potentialities which remain undeveloped if they live in isolation.

The first society is the family, and modern experience has re-convinced many who needed to be reconvinced that the only model of the family that will serve society adequately is that which is based on faithful monogamy, the parents being committed to caring for their children and educating them in the ways of civilised living, and the children being taught by example to love and obey them. It is unfortunately true that, for various reasons, many children will be born into and grow up in circumstances that are far from that ideal. Society must do all it can to see that such children suffer as little as possible, by helping their parents to help themselves, while doing all it can to provide the context in which the model of the family can flourish.

The family in its turn needs to relate to and co-operate with other families; in doing so it builds up civil society. In simple societies it can do this in the tribal form, which is based on blood relationships, and has certain political functions. Where civil society has developed beyond this model, growing in complexity and size in a manner which weakens any ties of blood and natural community that there may originally have been, it needs to develop into political society, choosing its own rulers and form of government to secure the common good.

The third principle is that man is born into freedom and for freedom[1]. Made in God's image and likeness, he must be able to obey God's law in freedom. In this way he can be happy in this life and, when life is over, receive the reward of eternal life. He must therefore have political and economic freedom, because only through them can he make the free choices in his life which will enable him to serve God worthily.

The fourth principle is that freedom, in order to be worthy of man's dignity as a child of God, must be lived according to God's law, known to him through his conscience, which is both objective and subjective. The *objective*, true conscience is a reflection in one's consciousness – one's intellect and will – of the law of God. True and objective conscience cannot err because it does not *make* its own moral law, but rather *reflects* God's law. It is schooled and formed in God's objective truth, which it then applies to specific circumstances. The *subjective* conscience is the faculty, the power of intellect and will, which enables man to apply the objective law of God to particular circumstances. Because it is subjective, because it is the individual's judgement and will, it can err through ignorance or through conditioning in evil by outside influences. It can also err by the decision to close the mind to a moral truth that could be known if the individual so wished.

Man is made in God's image, possessing understanding and free will

God created man in his own image and likeness, endowed him with free will and intelligence and made him Lord of creation. 'Thou hast made him little less than the angels, set him over the work of thy hands'. [*Pacem in Terris* 3]

The Church's social teaching rests on one basic principle: individual human beings are the foundation, the cause and the end of every social institution. [*Mater et Magistra* 218–219]

The primordial assertion of the Church's anthropology is that the human being is the image of God and cannot be reduced to a mere fragment of nature or an anonymous element in the human city.
[John Paul II, *Puebla,* CIIR, London 1980, p. 7]

Christ is the perfect man who has restored in the children of Adam the likeness of God. By his incarnation he, the son of God, has, in a certain way, united himself with each man. He worked with human hands, he thought with a human mind, acted with a human will and with a human heart he loved. [*Redemptor Hominis* 8]

Man is by nature social

Experience of his own weakness both impels and encourages a man to ally his forces with those of another in political society and in other societies. These are called private societies because their purpose is the particular interest of their own members. The state does not possess the power to make a general order against their existence.
[*Rerum Novarum* 49–50]

The social nature of man shows that there is an interdependence between personal betterment and the improvement of society. Man by his very nature stands in need of life in society. Life in society is not something accessory to man himself; through his dealings with others, through mutual service and through fraternal dialogue, man develops all his talents and becomes able to rise to his destiny. [*Gaudium et Spes* 25]

Man is free under the law of God

Man's personal dignity requires that he enjoy freedom to make up his own mind. Man should act on his own initiative, conviction and sense of responsibility, not under constant pressure of external coercion. We should think of human society as being primarily a spiritual reality. Its foundation is truth, brought into effect by justice, perfected by love. Such an order finds its source in the true, personal and transcendent God. [*Pacem in Terris* 34, 36–38]

Revelation teaches that the power to decide what is evil and what is good does not belong to man but to God alone. Human freedom is not

.

---

unlimited for it is called to accept the moral law given by God who alone is good and knows what is good for man. [*Veritatis Splendor* 35]

Man knows the good through his conscience

This good is established by the eternal law known by man's natural reason [natural law] and by God's supernatural revelation [divine positive law]. [*Veritatis Splendor* 72]

In the depth of his conscience, man detects a law which holds him to obedience. It does not establish the law. In the case of a correct conscience, objective truth is achieved. Error of conscience can be the result of ignorance. Evil done as a result may not be imputable, but it does not cease to be an evil. Conscience compromises its dignity when man shows little concern for what is true and good and becomes almost blind from being accustomed to sin. [*Veritatis Splendor* 54–63]

3. The Family – the foundation of Church and Society

God is the author of marriage

The intimate partnership of life and love that is the married state has been established by the Creator . . . it is rooted in the contract of the partners, that is in their irrevocable personal consent, confirmed by divine law, receiving its stability from the human act by which the partners surrender themselves to each other. It excludes adultery and divorce. [*Gaudium et Spes* 48, 49]

Marriage and married love are ordered to giving life and nurturing it

By its very nature the institution of marriage and married love is ordered to the procreation and education of offspring. The intimate union, as a mutual giving of two persons, and the good of the children, demands total fidelity from spouses. Authentic married love is caught up into divine love. Inspired by the example of their parents, children and everyone under the family roof will more easily set out on the path of truly human training, of holiness. Children are the supreme gift of marriage. Married couples should regard it as their proper mission to transmit life. [*Gaudium et Spes* 48, 50]

Marriage and family are undermined by sexual permissiveness

The family is the most important and basic of human societies, and it is founded on the sexual love between man and woman from which love new human life is born. 'The creator from the beginning made them male and female. This is why a man must leave father and mother and cling to his wife and the two become one body.' [*Matthew* 19:5]. The sons of God 'looking on the daughters of men saw they were pleasing' [*Genesis* 6:2], married and had children by them. There is no biblical teaching on sex as such; there is a teaching on marriage of which it is part. Marriage is to be monogamous, faithful and lifelong. The two are one flesh and cannot be put asunder – and it is to be a fruitful love. Through marriage new life comes into being: with children raised by loving parents, who educate them with the support of society, to live by the standards that make good citizens, that society can be assured of a healthy future. Parents are to decide how many children they should have, in the light of their duty to God, to themselves, their families and society. Where children cannot be born of a marriage, however, married love remains a good. The very sadness that couples who are infertile feel, heightens the realisation of the link between love and the giving of life. Giving themselves generously to one another in love, they feel deeply the anguish that they cannot generate new life. It is one of the many sadnesses of the human condition that good people who would cherish new life born of them should suffer in this way; it is tragic also that in the effort to overcome the problem, methods are sometimes used that undermine the dignity of the parents, turn human life into a commodity, and could cause severe problems for the children they might conceive.

   It is necessary that family life be stable and respected, to defend the dignity, the privilege and responsibilities of sex by the virtue of chastity. The Christian teaching here seems very hard. Based on *Genesis* 1:24–28, 2:18–24, 3:16–24 and *Matthew* 19:3–12, it tells us that sex is for marriage only. Male and female he created them and the two become one flesh; it is this coming together in love which seals the marriage bond in lifelong fidelity. Any other form of sexual act between persons is excluded by this law. It is the virtue of chastity that enables us to integrate our sexuality with our total personality. For those who are not married, this means total abstinence from free sexual acts. For those who are married it means using their sexual faculties in a way which is worthy; in particular, both the unitive and the procreative aspects of the sexual act must be preserved in each and every act. Sex in marriage without love denies its unitive aspect. Sex in marriage which deliberately denies conception at a time when conception is possible (approximately one week in four) denies the Creator's procreative plan. The reasons why many Catholics today reject this traditional and constant teaching are many and complex; objective evil is often done by those whose moral imputability for it is limited, but objective evil it remains: it demeans the dignity of those who act this way and tolerance of such evil eventually corrupts society as a whole – as we see from experience.

This teaching runs completely counter to our culture, but we must remind ourselves that it has never been the Christian way to look first to what the world says. The sexual ethics that the Church expects of us are those which she has always taught and always will teach because they embody Gospel values. Millions of Christians, today just as in the past, live happily, more happily, because they live by them. It makes sense to do so. Firstly, it keeps us faithful to the Lord who gave us life. Secondly, it preserves our human dignity. Sex is a good if it is subject to the control of grace and reason. Otherwise we degrade ourselves by its misuse. Thirdly, it prevents injustice to others: to those whom we would be tempted to abuse by casual sex, to their parents, spouses, siblings or children who would be affected by such behaviour, to the diseases we might visit on others because of our profligacy, to the illegitimate children we might father or bear.

It is also apparent from our experience of the permissive society, that casting aside all sexual restraint does not make for lasting personal happiness, but leads to man and woman using one another as objects, which degrades both of them. At the same time it is supremely anti-social because it undermines the family, with all that that means for the future of society. The overwhelming experience of the breakdown of the model family over the last forty years or so is that it is a tragedy for children and those members of the extended family pattern who are weak or old. Children need a father and a mother who are pledged to lifelong fidelity and who are committed to their proper upbringing. Society must give them every support in this. That an increasing number of children are being born into families not of this kind imposes on the public authorities and on all of us the obligation to do what we can to help these children, and to help their parents to help themselves. The innocent victims of broken families, or victims of other personal tragedies, should not be made to feel that they are second-class people; they have a right to respect, love and care. At the same time, we must not make the mistake of failing to hold up the model family as society's ideal and norm on account of our sympathy for those who do not enjoy membership of one. On the contrary, everything that can be done should be done to rekindle trust in it. Christian sexual morality is essential to this: it keeps us faithful to God the giver of life, it makes sex subject to grace and reason and so a positive force in our lives, it prevents us inflicting injustice on others whom we would abuse by casual sex, and it instils in us the values that support the family and all its members.

The questions of infertility and family planning

Even where, despite the intense desire of the spouses, there are no children, marriage retains its character of being a whole manner and communion of life. Married people sometimes find themselves in a position where the number of children cannot be increased. Life must be protected with the utmost care from the moment of conception. Abortion and infanticide are abominable crimes. In questions of birth regulation, sons of the Church are forbidden to use those disapproved by the teaching of the Church in its interpretation of the divine law. [*Gaudium et Spes* 50, 51; *Humanae Vitae* 8–16]

Periodic continence, based on self-observation and the use of infertile periods, is in conformity with objective criteria of morality respecting the bodies of the spouses, encouraging tenderness, and authentic freedom. In contrast, every action which, whether in anticipation of the conjugal

act, or in its accomplishment, or in the development of its natural consequences, proposes, whether as an end or as a means, to render procreation impossible, is intrinsically evil.
[*Catechism of the Catholic Church* 2370]

The Family is the foundation of Society and the Church

The family is the place where the different generations come together and help one another to grow wiser and harmonise the rights of individuals with the demands of social life: as such it constitutes the basis of society. [*Gaudium et Spes* 52]

Spouses, when they are given the dignity of fatherhood and motherhood carry out their duties of education. Children, with gratitude, affection and trust, repay their parents for the benefits given them and will come to their assistance in the loneliness of old age. Widowhood will be honoured by all. The active presence of the father is necessary for the training of children. The mother has a central role; this role must be safeguarded without underrating women's legitimate social advancement. The civil authority should consider it a sacred duty to acknowledge the true nature of the family. It devolves on priests to be properly trained to deal with family matters by pastoral means. [*Gaudium et Spes* 48, 52]

The Creator established the conjugal relationship as the basis of society; it is from the family that citizens come to birth and it is within the family that they find the first school of the social virtues that are the animating principles of society itself. The family is also the Church in miniature, the domestic church. [*Familiaris Consortio* 42, 49]

Society should never fail in its fundamental task of respecting and fostering the family. Family and society have complementary functions in defending the good of each and every human being. Society, specifically the state, must recognise that the family is a society in its own right and must not take away from families those functions they can just as well perform for themselves; the public authorities must ensure that families have the economic, social, educational and cultural assistance they need. [*Familiaris Consortio* 45]

The family is placed at the service of the building up of the kingdom of God by participating in the life and mission of the Church. The pastoral intervention of the Church in the support of the family is a matter of urgency: more necessary than ever is the preparation of young people for marriage and family life. In her pastoral care of families the Church must help them harmonise the intimacy of home life with the work of building up the Church and society. [*Familiaris Consortio* 49, 65, 66]

4. Civil society and intermediate organisations

The Christian understanding of man and society in the first stage of the latter's development, is that morally responsible individuals and families co-operate with one another in the tasks of social organisation beyond the family. Building up a model or theory of this civil (but not political) society, persons and families form associations which are voluntary. They found villages, settlements, towns. They combine for economic purposes, and organise the various sectors of the economy – farming, commerce, industry. They also join with others in cultural or religious pursuits. As society becomes more complex, it becomes less informal and it requires the rule of law so that conflicts of interest, protection from external enemies and positive action for the common good can be taken. Civil society has, in other words, generated the need for political society which can make and enforce law for the common good.

Intermediate organisations, those which are founded by private initiative, not by the initiative of the state, retain and increase their importance in political society. The state's role is subsidiary, helping intermediate organisations when they need it, not replacing them. Political structures have their own autonomy, function and purpose and they affect all areas of life. But they should not dominate them. On the contrary, they must allow, approve and encourage private initiative such as: business organisations and operations, companies, financial and economic enterprises, industrial and commercial activities, trades unions and employers' associations, private educational and medical services on a regional or national scale, voluntary charitable organisations, cultural and professional associations, the arts and sciences, political parties, publishing, the media, entertainments and sporting activities.

Men have the right to form associations and give them the form which they consider most suitable for their objectives. Such organisations safeguard man's personal freedom and dignity. [*Pacem in Terris* 23–24]

The social nature of man is realised in the intermediary groups, beginning with the family and including economic, social, political and cultural groups which stem from human nature itself and have their own autonomy, always with a view to the common good.
[*Centesimus Annus* 13]

Numerous intermediary bodies and corporate enterprises are the main vehicle of social growth. They collaborate in the pursuit of their own specific interests and those of the common good.
[*Mater et Magistra* 65–7]

5. Community and civil society: Solidarity

The distinction between community and society is one on which some sociologists have spilt much ink. One does not have to be a purist to see that there is something in it; but it must not be pressed too far. 'Community' suggests an organisation based on natural dispositions that spring from common racial characteristics, stable united social groups or those which base themselves on an ideal that itself produces social cohesion. 'Society' suggests something more formal, something that need not be the product of slow growth, but may arise almost instantaneously if necessary, and which is bound together in a more formal way, if not by law (political society) then at least by some convention ratified informally or by implication (civil society). In fact, community and society tend to blend into one another and it is impossible to distinguish them completely, in theory or in practice. Even the least formal group requires in it some principle of organisation and authority, whilst even the most formal will have in it something of the informal.

Solidarity

Human society, civic or political, needs a principle of unity that goes beyond simple self-interest. Self-interest is important; the love we have for ourselves is the measure of how we should love others. Unfortunately, this second aspect of it is often forgotten: self-interest becomes abusive of the rights of others. There needs to be an agreed set of values which will underpin the law and frame sound social institutions to offset this innate selfishness. These can be provided, for example, by common racial origins, strong cultural or compatible multicultural conditions, historical experience, or a combination of all three. In theory, the soundest basis for such solidarity is the truth that the whole human race is made in God's image and likeness, and that all men and women are therefore entitled to be treated accordingly, to be given their rights and be expected to accept their responsibilities as sons and daughters of God. The unfortunate truth is that those who believe in this *in theory* have often shown that they are unable effectively to put it into practice. In this we can see how weak and unstable human nature is.

It remains true that it is only the transcendent dimension, the belief that there is a power above us to which we are subject of our natures, which can provide the framework within which common humanity can be expected to accept the restraints on human selfishness required by a healthy society. We cannot avoid our obligation as Christians to keep this truth before society. We must remember that this is not only a Christian insight: it is an insight which the Stoic philosophers arrived at, as have many of the non-Christian religions of the world. That non-believers and believers who are of this mind often disagree on how they should work in society to see this truth become a reality, does not invalidate the truth in itself. It is a cultural, not a political, gift. It is certainly true that solidarity must grow out of something other than political policy. States have a duty to try to encourage solidarity, but political philosophies, which deal with the ordering of this world primarily, cannot alone explain why solidarity should exist. These must come from beliefs and traditions which accept the transcendent and make it the measure of human purpose and happiness.

Scripture tells us how God made us in his own image and likeness. This is a marvellous vision which enables us to see the human race in the one common origin in God. Christ commanded us to love one another as he had loved us. In this perspective individuals are not isolated like grains of sand, but united by their very nature and eternal destiny.
[*Summi Pontificatus* 36–42]

The exercise of solidarity within each society is valid when its citizens recognise each other as persons. Those who are more influential because they have a greater share of goods and common services should feel a sense of responsibility for the weaker and be ready to share with them all that they possess. Those who are weaker, for their part, in the same spirit of solidarity, should not adopt a purely passive attitude or one that is destructive of the social fabric, but, while claiming their legitimate rights, should do what they can for the good of all. The intermediate groups, for their part, should not selfishly insist on their particular interests, but respect the interests of others.
[*Sollicitudo Rei Socialis* 39]

Solidarity is the direct requirement of human and supernatural brotherhood. The serious socio-economic problems which occur today cannot be solved unless new fronts of solidarity are created: solidarity of the poor among themselves, solidarity with the poor to which the rich are called, solidarity among the workers and with the workers. Institutions and social organisations at different levels, as well as the state, must share in the general movement of solidarity. When the Church appeals for such solidarity, she is aware that she herself is concerned in quite a special way. [*Libertatis Conscientia* 89]

Justice in society and unjust social structures

The modern social documents only deal in passing with the nature of social, political and economic justice, but when they do so they refer most often to St Thomas' treatment of the subject, so we will follow him.

Justice is a habit whereby a man renders to each one his due by constant and perpetual will. Just as love of God includes love of neighbour, so too the service of God includes rendering to each one his due.
[*Summa Theologica* IIa IIae Q 58 Art 1 ad 6]

General justice (which can equally well be called legal justice (i.e. in the law) or social justice (justice in society in general)) is concerned with the common good:

> . . . and thus it is in the sovereign [i.e. the ruler, the government] principally and by way of a master craft while it is secondarily in his subjects [i.e. in so far as they have to obey just laws].
> [*Summa Theologica* IIa IIae Q 58 Art 6]

The distribution of property and regulation of possessions is a major concern of the ruler whose duty it is to see that all have access to the necessities of life because this is required for virtue; the absence of justice in economic life is a cause of social disorder:

> As the Philosopher says, the regulation of possessions conduces much to the preservation of the state or nation.
> [*Summa Theologica* Ia IIae Q 105 art 2 ad 3]

> It is necessary that there be through the ruler's sagacity a sufficiency of those goods which are indispensable for well-being.
> [*De Regimine Principum* 1.15]

Men come together in society to find the means to sustain their existence, and the ruler (who could only be the Prince in the cultural epoch in which St Thomas lived) has the duty to secure the common good, so he must organise his realm in such a way that the needs of a decent existence are available for all his people (it being assumed, of course, that they will work hard and well to secure it). [A P D'Entrèves, *Aquinas: Selected Political Writings*, Oxford 1948, pp 79ff; W J MacDonald, *The Social Value of Property according to St Thomas Aquinas*, Washington DC 1939, pp 42ff].

Besides General [or Legal or Social] Justice there is *particular* justice, firstly commutative, economic justice in exchange of goods by barter or selling; and here there must be exact equivalence between what is agreed and what is paid. Secondly, there is distributive justice which is concerned with the distribution of the goods and honours of the State among its citizens according to their contribution to the commonweal.

> Commutative justice is concerned with the mutual dealings between two people while distributive justice distributes common goods proportionately. In commutations something is paid to an individual chiefly in buying and selling. Hence it is necessary to equalise thing with thing – equality in *arithmetical* proportion. In distributive justice we find equality in *geometric* proportion; a person's station is considered.
> [*Summa Theologica* IIa IIae Q 61 Art 1, Art 2]

Justice at all levels is the mark of a sound and healthy society, but justice alone cannot knit society together: it needs to be given in a context of love, of charity.

> Peace is the work of justice indirectly insofar as justice removes the obstacles to peace; but it is the work of charity directly because charity, according to its very nature, causes peace. For love is a unitive force and peace is the union of the appetite's inclinations.
> [*Summa Theologica* IIa IIae Q 29 Art 3 ad 3]

Where unjust structures exist in society, then the Christian must work peacefully for change. However, this change will not be achieved unless the hearts and minds of those who perpetrate injustices are changed also, otherwise the injustices will simply reappear in a different form. This can be demonstrated by revolutions that produce more injustice than that which they set out to counter, or where populist demagogues are elected on rash promises which simply lead to a greater exploitation of the hardworking, the weak and the poor.

> It is perfectly legitimate that those who suffer persecution by the wealthy or the politically powerful should take action through morally legitimate means, in order to secure structures and institutions in which their rights will be truly respected. It remains true, however, that it is necessary to work simultaneously for the conversion of hearts and for the improvement of structures, for the sin which is at the root of unjust structures is, in a true and immediate sense, a voluntary act which has its source in the freedom of individuals. Only in a derived and secondary sense is it applicable to structures, and only in this sense can we speak of 'structures of sin'. [*Libertatis Conscientia* 75]

> Moral evil, the fruit of many sins, leads to structures of sin. To diagnose the evil in this way is to identify precisely, on the level of human conduct,

the path to be followed in order to overcome it. The obstacles to integral development are not only economic but rest on more profound attitudes. [*Sollicitudo Rei Socialis* 37–38]

Human rights and responsibilities

Because all mankind is made in God's image and likeness, there should be no injustice to anyone on the grounds of race, background, religion, culture, sex, or on account of any other prejudice. Justice is about rights and about backing them up by law, but not all human rights can be backed up in this way. There is a right to work, but it is not feasible to make it enforceable at law; there is also a right to an education commensurate with ability, but not all societies have the means to make it available to all capable of receiving it.

There are some rights which must be guaranteed at law, the right to life being the most obvious one. It is a commentary on the morality of the secular liberalism which now rules our society that this right is no longer guaranteed – because of abortion on demand and the increasing pressure to make what is euphemistically called 'euthanasia' legal.

These challenges to the most basic of human rights remind us how important it is to keep in mind what those rights are, and what their basis is for the Christian. That basis is not feelings (even right feelings), convention, the positive law, or the consensus of a secular liberal society which has lost its moral compass. Properly considered, human rights derive from man's dignity as a being made in God's image and likeness; man is given intelligence and free will so that he can choose the good, the good made known through the objective law of God. For those who do not know the one true God, this good is known through the natural law. For those who do know God, the good is known by Revelation and the Church which interprets it. Secular liberalism, which in the last analysis is individualistic selfishness, cannot provide this understanding.

God's law requires respect for human rights: it excludes racialism

Peace on earth depends on the observance of the divine order. The Father has inscribed in man's nature how to behave towards his fellow man. Each individual is a person, with intelligence and free will, and has rights and duties which flow from his nature. These rights are universal and inviolable. Men have been ransomed by the blood of Jesus Christ; Grace has made them sons and friends of God, heirs to eternal glory. [*Pacem in Terris* 1–10]

Victims of injustice are those who are discriminated against in law or in fact on account of their race, origin, colour, culture, sex, or religion. Racial discrimination possesses a character of very great relevance by reason of the tension which it stirs up. The members of mankind share the same basic rights and duties as well as the same supernatural destiny. [*Octogesima Adveniens* 16]

The rights of man, human rights

1.   *Man has a right to live,* to bodily integrity and the means necessary for proper development, to food, clothing, medical care, rest, necessary social services, care in ill health, in disability stemming from his work, in widowhood, old age, unemployment or whenever through no fault of his own he is deprived of the means of livelihood.

2.   *He has a right to be respected,* to a good name, to freedom in investigating the truth, and – within the limits of the moral order and the common good – to freedom of speech and publication, to pursue whatever profession he may choose, to be accurately informed about public events.

3.   *He has the right to the benefits of culture,* a good general education, technical or professional training consistent with the degree of educational development in his own country, to engage in advanced studies, to (as far as possible) positions of responsibility commensurate with his talent and skill.

4.   *Among man's rights is that of being able to worship God according to his conscience* and profess his religion in private and in public.

5.   *Human beings also have the right to choose for themselves the life which appeals to them,* to marry and found a family, in which man and women have equal rights; or not to marry.

6. *Man has the right to the opportunity to work* and to take personal initiative in it. Conditions in it must not be such as to weaken physical or moral fibre.

7. *Man has a right to engage in economic activities suited to his degree of responsibility*; to a wage in accordance with justice; to ownership of private property, including productive goods.

8. *Men have a right to form associations with their fellows,* to confer on such associations the type of organisation best calculated to achieve their aims.

9. *Every human being has the right to freedom of movement and residence in his own state* and, where just reasons favour it, to emigrate to other countries.

10. *Man has a right to take an active part in public life,* to make his own contribution to the common welfare.

11. *As a human person he is entitled to the legal protection of his rights,* effective, unbiased and just. [*Pacem in Terris* 11–27]

With these rights go duties

To claim one's rights and ignore one's duties is like building a house with one hand and tearing it down with the other. The right to life involves the duty to preserve one's life, and the right to a decent standard of living, the duty to live in a becoming fashion; the right to be free brings with it the duty to seek out the truth and to devote oneself to an ever deeper and wider search for it, and to recognise one's rights and duties The result will be that each individual makes his wholehearted contribution to the creation of a civic order in which rights and duties are ever more diligently and effectively observed.
[*Pacem in Terris* 30, 29, 31]

Man's personal dignity requires that he enjoy freedom. His recognition of rights, observance of duties, and collaboration with other men should be a matter of his own personal decision, his own initiative, conviction and sense of responsibility. [*Pacem in Terris* 34]

Human society demands that men be guided by justice, respect the rights of others and do their duty. They must feel the needs of others as their own. So considered, we think of society as primarily a spiritual reality.

Its foundation is truth, brought into effect by justice. Such an order, absolute, immutable in its principles, finds its source in the true personal and transcendent God, who is the first truth and the highest good, the deepest source from which human society can draw its genuine vitality. [*Pacem in Terris* 35–38]

6. Social class and social conflict

Christian and Marxist views

The Christian view of society is not egalitarian; that there should be differences in fortune and prosperity between people is accepted in both the Old and the New Testaments. But it is also part of Judaeo-Christian belief that all men and women are equal in human dignity, and that the wealth of the world was given to mankind in order that all might enjoy a good life from it, so the degree of inequality in society should not be so great that it means there is social injustice. The earth should yield the necessities of a decent life for all who are prepared to work for it.

Neither does the Christian assume that existing patterns of the distribution of wealth are necessarily just. It is always acceptable to ask whether a particular form of distribution respects the common good, and if it does not, to work peacefully and under the law to change it. It is the state which has the right and the duty to see that justice is done in these matters, but that justice does not mean that some cannot be wealthier than others. If they gain their wealth honestly and use it in accordance with just law then they are entitled to keep it and enjoy it. In particular they can own productive goods and work them for profit, again assuming that this is under just law.

The injustices of the liberal capitalist industrial revolution, however, convinced Karl Marx in the nineteenth century that private ownership of productive goods should be abolished, and he claimed to have discovered the scientific laws governing human society which would ensure that it would.

These laws opposed class to class, and the end result of this opposition would be the inevitable uprising of those without property, the proletariat, the demise of the capitalist and, by some means never exactly explained, the state would wither away, and the social ownership of the means of production would ensure economic justice. The Church did not deny that there had been gross injustice under liberal capitalism. But she said that the answer was not the abolition of private ownership of productive goods, and of the capitalist class, but the right moral principles, and the action of the State, the employers and the employed to remove the causes of injustice in order to build a more just society.

Reconciling class to class; charity and justice; the preferential option for the poor

Rerum Novarum, issued by Pope Leo XIII in 1891, was the first major document of the Church which confronted the situation in liberal capitalist industry in Europe and North America. Some thought the judgement on the system too severe, but no responsible commentator denied that a grave injustice had been done.

> Working men are now left isolated and helpless, betrayed by the inhumanity of employers and the unbridled greed of competitors. A tiny group of extravagantly rich men have been able to lay upon a great multitude of unpropertied workers a yoke little better than slavery itself. [*Rerum Novarum* 2]

But labour and capital are not natural enemies:

> Each stands entirely in need of the other; there can be no capital without labour nor labour without capital. [*Rerum Novarum* 16]

Overwhelmingly, the defects of the system were laid at the door of the Liberal capitalists and the economic interests they represented. The unpropertied worker

> must fulfil faithfully and complete whatever contract of employment he has freely and justly made; do no damage to the property nor harm the person of his employers; to refrain from the use of force in defence of his own interests and inciting civil discord. [*Rerum Novarum* 17]

For the rest, the document is an indictment of the way in which liberal capitalism, and states controlled by it, had seriously offended against justice, thus creating the social problem.

> The first task is to save workers from the brutality of those who make use of human beings as mere instruments in the creation of wealth, impose a burden of labour which stupefies minds and exhausts bodies. Let workers and employers make bargains freely about wages, but there underlies a requirement of natural justice higher and older than any bargain; a wage ought not to be insufficient for needs.
> [*Rerum Novarum* 43, 45]

Solidarity was the key:

> All men have the same Father who is God the Creator, the same benefits of nature and gifts of divine grace belong in common to the whole human race: 'we are children, we are heirs as well; heirs of God and co-heirs with Christ'. [*Rerum Novarum* 24]

It must have practical results, and the Church has a part to play:

> She wants to see the unpropertied workers emerge from their great poverty and better their condition. [*Rerum Novarum* 28].

Employers and workers can and must co-operate in the improvement of the lot of the latter: experience has shown that

> Employers and workers can do much themselves to bring timely aid to the needy and draw class closer to class; examples are mutual benefit societies. [*Rerum Novarum* 48]

But most important are:

> Working men's associations and unions of workers must bring to their members as great as possible an increase in physical and spiritual well-being and access to property. Christians can form unions of their own. [*Rerum Novarum* 48, 56, 58]

The state has a crucial role:

> Authority must intervene when the public interest or that of a particular class is harmed, if this is the only way to remove the evil. Rich people can protect themselves; the poor have to depend above all upon the

state. Because the wage earners are numbered among the multitude of the poor, the State owes them particular care and protection.
[*Rerum Novarum* 37, 38]

The option or love of preference for the poor is an option or special form of primacy in the exercise of Christian charity to which the Tradition of the Church bears witness. Today the world-wide dimension of the social problem cannot but embrace the multitude of the hungry, the needy, above all those without hope. [*Sollicitudo Rei Socialis* 42]

The special option for the poor, far from being a sign of particularism or sectarianism, manifests the universality of the Church's being and mission. This option excludes no one. This is why the Church cannot express this option by the means of reductive categories which would make this preference a partisan choice and a source of conflict.
[*Libertatis Conscientia* 68]

7. Community and civil society: subsidiarity

That the citizen has rights which the state cannot take away from him, and that man is the end and purpose of every social organisation, are principles which a healthy civil society must foster. Citizens receive from their parents the essential moral education which makes them capable of using freedom for good and not for ill, and because of this ability they can claim their rights and meet their responsibilities. Freedom under the natural and the divine laws prevents freedom giving way to licence, and encourages independent-minded people capable of running their own affairs.

This strong sense of independence is not anti-communitarian or anti-social; solidarity with others is a basic social value since all are the children of God and have to be loved and respected as such. No man is an island. While ability to run one's own affairs and be independent is essential for the common good, this does not mean that persons, families and intermediate societies are not entitled to help from their fellow citizens when they need it. On the contrary, it is solidarity which demands it, and this is summed up in the concept of 'subsidiarity' [from the Latin *subsidium* which means 'help']. It states that persons, families and smaller organisations who need help in overcoming the problems which prevent them from fulfilling their potential, must be given it; the help given, and the manner in which it is given, should have the aim of making those who receive the help independent again as soon as possible.

The term was used first in the encyclical *Quadragesimo Anno* in 1931, but the obligation it indicated was in the law of the Old Testament in its injunctions to succour the widow, the orphan and the stranger in their need. In the New Testament it was highlighted by the parable of the Good Samaritan; and it has been present in the social welfare work of the Church throughout its history. In principle it was there in *Rerum Novarum,* where the duty of the State to care for the weak and the poor was especially stressed. Subsidiarity sums up the Christian obligation to help others in their need, when unemployment, poverty or serious sickness of any form prevent them from supporting themselves. However, since the aim of this help is to try to make people independent again, it should only be temporary; only those who cannot support themselves because of permanent serious illness, or on account of old age, can expect to be supported by the state permanently.

> It is an injustice and at the same time a great evil and disturbance of right order to assign to a greater and higher association what lesser and subordinate organisations can do. For every social activity ought of its very nature to furnish help to the members of the body social, and never destroy or absorb them. [*Quadragesimo Anno* 79]

> If there is one thing that we have learned from the school of experience it is this: that, in the modern world especially, political, economic and cultural inequalities among the citizens become more widespread when the public authorities fail to take appropriate action in those spheres. [*Pacem in Terris* 63]

> Neither the state nor any society must substitute itself for the initiative and responsibility of individuals or intermediate communities at the level at which they can function, nor must they take away the room necessary for their freedom. Hence the Church's social doctrine is opposed to all forms of collectivism. [*Libertatis Conscientia* 73]

Chapter Two
Ethics and Political Society

1. Introduction

The model of society as the Catholic tradition sees it, therefore, consists firstly of civil society, in which man develops in the context of the family; and then the family groups and individuals build up a pattern of organisations and associations for cultural, social and economic purposes. Governed as they are by the natural law and the divine revealed law, they establish their moral and spiritual values accordingly in harmony with the law of God, showing solidarity with others because of the belief that all are his children. In time, the need for political society makes itself felt as the population grows, and with it the demands of social organisation. Informal arrangements and conventions are no longer sufficient to secure the common good. Law is needed, and that implies the means of enforcing it. Community and civil society cannot perform these functions; state and government are needed, under a constitution which provides for freedom and human rights for all.

The citizen brings into this political society a notion of human rights, based on his being made in the image and likeness of God, having intelligence and free will, knowing the difference between right and wrong by right reason (natural law) and God's revealed law (through the Scriptures and the Church which interprets them). The citizen is therefore capable of the right use of freedom. The state must respect these human rights, support them and not undermine them. Other rights and obligations will arise out of the needs of political society; these must harmonise with the citizen's natural rights, and the citizens must help build up political society on the basis of the truth, justice and love.

Civil society and political society are complementary, not in opposition to one another. There will be tension between them at times because mankind is imperfect and perceptions of the common good differ. Respect for human rights, solidarity, subsidiarity, just law and government, and a sound social, legal, political and economic system can channel the tensions constructively towards a solution.

2. The origin, purpose and nature of political society

The state is founded in God and derives its authority from him

The Catholic tradition asserts that the right to rule is from God, as from a natural and necessary principle. [*Diuturnum Illud* 5]

The political authorities derive their authority from God. Is every ruler appointed by God? No, but his authority as such is. That a ruling authority should come about is a provision of divine wisdom.
[*Pacem in Terris* 46]

Representatives of the state have no power to bind men in conscience unless their own authority is tied to God's. Obedience to civil authority is in reality an act of homage paid to God. We do not demean ourselves in showing due reverence to God; we are lifted up and ennobled, for to serve God is to reign. [*Pacem in Terris* 49–50]

It must not be imagined that authority therefore has no bounds. Laws and decrees passed in contravention of the moral order are unjust and have no longer the rationale of law but are rather acts of violence.
[*Pacem in Terris* 47, 51]

The authority of the ruler comes not directly from God but through the people

The political power rests immediately, as in its subject, in the whole multitude of the people, for the power comes from God, and God, having assigned it to no particular man, must have given it to the multitude.
[Robert Bellarmine, *De Membris Ecclesiae,* quoted in James Brodrick SJ, *The Life and Work of Blessed Robert Bellarmine SJ, 1542–1621,* London 1928, Vol. 1, p 222]

It is obvious that it rests with the people as a whole to decide whether they should have a king, or consuls, or other magistrates. Furthermore the people can change their government from a monarchy to an aristocracy or democracy or the other way round. It is quite true that all power comes from God, but that of temporal princes is derived from God, not immediately but through the consent of human wills. [*Bellarmine*, Brodrick, p 222, 224]

Those who are placed over the state may be chosen by the will and decision of the multitude. The people are not hindered from choosing the government which suits them best. [*Diuturnum Illud* 6–7]

The common good, the purpose of the state, is achieved when all have their human rights

Individuals, families and the various groups which make up the civil community are aware of their inability to achieve a truly human life by their own efforts and set up political communities for the common good, which embraces the sum total of those conditions of social life which enable individuals, families and organisations to achieve complete and efficacious fulfilment. [*Gaudium et Spes* 74]

It is the nature of the common good that every single citizen has the right to share in it in a different way, depending on his tasks, merits and circumstances. Hence the civil authority must strive to promote the common good in the interest of all without favouring any category of citizen; justice and equity can however demand that it pay more attention to the weaker members. [*Pacem in Terris* 56]

The common good is best safeguarded when personal rights and duties are guaranteed. The chief concern of the civil authorities must be to ensure that these rights are recognised, respected and promoted. [*Pacem in Terris* 60]

The state's nature is positive: developing the individual and public well-being

Statesmanship consists in making the structure and administrative functioning of the State conduce to public and private prosperity: sound morals, family life, regard for religion and justice, moderate taxes equitably levied, growing industry and trade, a flourishing agriculture,

the greater well-being and happiness of the citizens.
[*Rerum Novarum* 33]

Government must not be thought of as a mere guardian of law and order, but rather must put forth every effort so that laws and institutions, public and individual well-being may develop spontaneously out of the structure and administration of the state. [*Quadragesimo Anno* 25]

Heads of States must make a positive contribution to the creation of a climate in which the individual can both safeguard his own rights and fulfil his duties, and ensure social as well as economic progress. The civil authorities must preserve a balance. The influence of the State must never be exerted to the extent of depriving the individual citizen of his freedom. It must augment his freedom while guaranteeing protection of everyone's rights. [*Pacem in Terris* 63–65]

Forms of State: the advantages of the people choosing their own rulers

All should have some share in government. Of the kinds of government, the best form of constitution is a mixture: of monarchy, in that one man is at the head; of aristocracy in that many rule as especially qualified; and of democracy in that the rulers can be chosen by the people and from them.
[St Thomas Aquinas, *Summa Theologica* Ia IIae Q 105 Art 1]

In determining what form government shall take, and the way in which it will function, a major consideration will be the prevailing circumstances and the condition of the people, and these are things which vary in different places and at different times. [*Pacem in Terris* 68]

The Church values the democratic system in as much as it ensures the participation of citizens in the making of political choices, and guarantees to those governed the possibility of both electing and holding accountable those who govern them and replacing them through peaceful means when appropriate. [*Centesimus Annus* 46]

Democracy cannot be idolised to the point of making it a substitute for morality or a panacea for immorality. Its moral value is not automatic but depends on its conformity to the moral law to which it, like every other form of human behaviour, must be subject. The value of democracy stands or falls by the standards which it embodies or promotes. [*Evangelium Vitae* 70]

The political responsibilities of the Christian

Every citizen should be mindful of his right and duty to promote the common good by using his vote. The Church praises and esteems those who devote themselves to the public good for the service of men and take upon themselves the burdens of office.

Among the duties of citizens it is worth mentioning the obligation of rendering to the state whatever material and personal services are required for the common good.

Christians must be conscious of their specific and proper role in the political community and be an example by their sense of responsibility and their dedication to the common good. They should recognise the legitimacy of different points of view about worldly affairs and show respect for their fellow citizens who defend their opinions by legitimate means. Those with a talent for the noble art of politics should engage in political activity with integrity, wisdom and courage.
[*Gaudium et Spes* 75]

3. Solidarity, subsidiarity and the political order

As we have seen, all nations and their social orders, if they are to flourish, require principles of unity which will enable the mass of citizens of every social class and background to cohere as a national community and provide an agreed set of values which will underpin the law and frame social institutions. States and political philosophies and parties have the duty to encourage solidarity, but they cannot of themselves create it. It must be the product of a vision of life which transcends that important sphere of secular life with which the state is concerned. It must be the product of a culture, of a philosophy or a theology which the state cannot control.

If solidarity can only be built out of a sound metaphysical or theological inheritance properly fostered by the state, subsidiarity is very much the fruit of the right sort of state action. We have seen that civil society, according to the Christian understanding of man's development, must be based on personal moral responsibility, fostered by the right values and founded on the eternal, revealed and natural laws, and through a healthy family life which fosters those values. In this context a capable and morally responsible citizenry can develop and groups can co-operate with one another in economic, social and cultural activities through patterns of associations in the pursuit of common aims. This civil society, ruled by agreed conventions and customs but not formal government, at some time realises that if the citizens are to achieve common aims peacefully and constructively, then laws that can be enforced are required. So political society emerges for that very purpose: to secure the common good, the good of each and the good of all.

The state and the government that administers it fosters that good by giving persons, families and private associations the maximum freedom compatible with the common good, and will only intervene in their affairs when they need help in achieving their aims. This necessary intervention should cease when they are capable of being independent again. The principle of 'subsidiarity' is the principle of necessary help, but only necessary help aimed at making persons, families and private associations independent once more. The State has a positive function, looking to foster the well-being of persons, families and private associations. Western nations from the late nineteenth century sought to relieve the poor living, working and cultural prospects of the wage earners that had been imposed on them during the industrial revolution under liberal capitalism. As they did so it was apparent that they had to encourage more sophisticated solutions to the social problem, and to arrange state intervention to provide for them where private initiative could not. By the 1950s the 'welfare state' had so expanded its activities that some guidance needed to be given on the moral issues involved.

The value of social assistance schemes, private and state

If there is one thing that we have learned from the school of experience, it is this: that, in the modern world especially, political, economic and cultural inequalities among the citizens become more widespread when the public authorities fail to take appropriate action in those spheres. [*Pacem in Terris* 63]

One of the principal characteristics typical of our age is mutual ties which grow daily more numerous. This development is at once a symptom and a cause of the growing intervention of the state and is not devoid of risk. Clearly it also brings many advantages in its train in what pertains to the necessities of life, health care, education, professional training, housing, work and suitable leisure and education. [*Mater et Magistra* 59–61]

Yet the means often used conspire to make it difficult for a person to think independently, to act on his own initiative. Must we conclude that men are necessarily reduced to the condition of being automatons? By no means. This growth is the creation of men who are free and autonomous by nature, though they cannot altogether escape from the pressure of their environment. [*Mater et Magistra* 62–3]

The dangers of the social assistance state

The common welfare demands that in their efforts to co-ordinate and protect the rights of citizens, the civil authorities preserve a delicate balance. They must not stand in the way of those rights. For this principle must always be retained: that however extensive and far-reaching the influence of the state may be, it must never be exerted at the expense of depriving the citizen of his freedom of action. It must rather augment his freedom. [*Pacem in Terris* 65]

The State has a right to intervene when social sectors are too weak. Such supplementary interventions are justified by urgent reasons touching the common good, but must be as brief as possible. Such interventions have remedied forms of poverty and deprivation unworthy of a human person. However, excesses and abuses have provoked very harsh criticisms of the welfare state. By depriving civil society of its responsibility, the social assistance state leads to a loss of human energies and an inordinate increase in public agencies accompanied by an enormous increase in spending. [*Centesimus Annus* 48]

4. The Common Good and party politics

The purpose of the state, therefore, is to secure the common good, but experience has shown that the only way to ensure the smooth functioning of democracy in major modern states is by representative government and regular elections. Those in their turn require political parties to organise so that, prior to elections, the electors can be presented with alternative policies to those of the government in office. Such parties also form alternative governments, having trained and able politicians ready to take over the office of State when elected.

By definition, the competing parties are urging different and opposing programmes. What then becomes of government for the common good? Provided there is a cultural coherence among the electorate, sharing the same value system or having compatible such systems, and agreeing on the nature of democratic government, it can be secured. If this coherence or agreement exists, political differences will be real but they will not be based on ideological differences so wide as to make impossible that compromise which is essential to the common good and democratic freedom. The problems of states which embrace irreconcilable ethnic differences illustrates the importance of practical solidarity and the dire consequences of its absence.

Christians must be tolerant of each other's different political opinions

Christians must recognise the legitimacy of different opinions with regard to temporal solutions, and respect citizens who, even as a group, defend their points of view by honest methods. [*Gaudium et Spes* 75]

In concrete situations, and taking account of the solidarity in each person's life, one must recognise a legitimate variety of possible options. The same Christian faith can lead to different commitments. The Church asks an effort at mutual understanding of the other's position and motives:

a loyal examination of one's behaviour and its correctness will suggest to each one an attitude of profound charity. [*Octogesima Adveniens* 50]

Moral principles and party politics: the Church is not to be made partisan

Political parties for their part must promote those things which in their judgement are required for the common good; it is never allowable to give their interests priority over the common good.
[*Gaudium et Spes* 75]

Secular duties and activities belong properly to laymen. They will gladly work with men seeking the same goals. They should know that it is the function of their well formed Christian consciences to see that the divine law is inscribed in the life of the earthly city. No one is allowed to appropriate the Church's authority for his opinion. They should try to enlighten one another through honest discussion, caring above all for the common good. [*Gaudium et Spes* 43]

It is important in a pluralistic society that there be a correct notion of the relationship between the political community and the Church, and a clear distinction between the tasks which Christians undertake, individually or as a group, on their own responsibility as citizens guided by the dictates of a Christian conscience, and the activities which, in union with their pastors, they carry out in the name of the Church. [*Gaudium et Spes* 76]

Christians who take up political activity should try to make their choices consistent with the Gospel and, in the framework of a legitimate plurality, to give witness to the seriousness of their faith by effective and disinterested service of man. [*Octogesima Adveniens* 46]

5. Law, morality, the common good, justice and human rights

Law, morality, justice, the common good and human rights are inter-linked in the Christian understanding of things. The purpose of the law is to give justice, to see that each gets what is his due; we know what is just because the moral law of God instructs us. The common good means the good of each and the good of all. And we can see that good is being achieved when all have their human rights. These too are founded in God's law; being made in God's image and likeness; all men must be treated according to that dignity.

Society must be rooted in freedom, guided by justice and animated by love. Human society in this perspective is primarily a spiritual reality through which men can share their knowledge of the truth, claim their rights and fulfil their duties. Such an order can only come through belief in universal, absolute and immutable good, based on belief in the one, true, personal and transcendent God, and his eternal, revealed and natural laws. The eternal law is in the mind of God and it gives to the created world and all creatures their rightful place in his plan. The natural law is implanted in man's mind and it reflects in that mind God's fundamental moral law, but, because of the uncertainty of human judgement, he also needs a revealed moral law – in the Scriptures and the Church's Tradition.

The eternal law of God is the basis of the social moral order

Such an order – universal, absolute and immutable in its principles – finds its source in the true, personal, and transcendent God. Human reason is the standard which measures the degree of goodness in the human will, and as such it derives from the eternal law, which is divine reason. [*Pacem in Terris* 38]

The whole universe is governed by divine reason. The very idea of the government of things in God, the ruler of the universe, has the nature of a law, and since the Divine Reason's conception of it is eternal, that law is eternal. [St Thomas Aquinas, *Summa Theologica* Ia IIae Q 91 Art 1]

The natural law is the immediate basis of political morality and human rights

The light of natural reason, by which we discern what is good and what is evil, is nothing else than an imprint of the divine reason, the sharing in the eternal law by intelligent creatures.
[*Summa Theologica* Ia IIae Q 91 Art 2]

The first precept of the natural law is that good is to be done and evil avoided. Other precepts derive from the tendency towards the good of one's nature. Firstly, Man has an instinct to preserve his own being; secondly, towards the coupling of male and female and the bringing up of young; thirdly, an appetite for the rational, the truths about God and about living in society – to shun ignorance, not to offend others and other related requirements. [*Summa Theologica* Ia IIae Q 94 Art 2]

The Father has inscribed in man's nature how to behave to his fellow men. Each individual is a person, with intelligence and free will, has rights and duties which flow from his nature. [*Pacem in Terris* 1–10]

The divine revealed moral law guides uncertain human judgement

On account of the uncertainty of human judgement . . . it was necessary for man to be directed in his proper acts by a law given by God, for it is certain that such a law cannot err.
[*Summa Theologica* Ia IIae Q 91 Art 4]

Totalitarianism debases man, and morally relativist democracy tends to totalitarianism

The so-called pre-Christian Germanic concept of God denies the wisdom and providence of God. What is morally indefensible can never contribute to the good of the people. Man as a person has rights he holds from God and which any collectivity must protect. To neglect this order is to shake the pillars on which society rests.
[*Mit Brennender Sorge* 7, 30]

The sphere of economics needs some morality, which can find no place in a system so thoroughly materialistic as communism. Terrorism is the only possible substitute. Society cannot defraud man of his God-granted rights. Communism inverts the terms of the relation of man to society.
[*Divini Redemptoris* 23, 30]

There is a tendency to claim that agnosticism and sceptical relativism correspond to democratic forms of political life. Yet if there is no ultimate truth, a democracy easily turns into open or thinly disguised totalitarianism. [*Centesimus Annus* 46]

6. Political dissent beyond party politics

Not all legitimate differences of opinion can find an effective outlet
through party politics and the formal procedures of democracy.
Democratic states allow peaceful public demonstration by private
associations on specific issues, subject to the protesters' meeting the
needs of reasonable public order. Where protesting on certain issues –
for example racial, religious, ethnic, trade union rights, abortion, nuclear
weapons, unpopular wars – leads to uncontrollable violence, the state
has a right and a duty, in an even-handed way, to ask the protesters to
find non-confrontational ways of making their point, and to make sure
that they adhere to them; but the principle of the right of public protest
must not be abandoned because some have abused the right in the
past. The right of conscientious objection to the shedding of blood is
another case of dissent that crosses party lines; the state has a duty to
tolerate those who have this objection, provided they make a peaceful
contribution to the cause of a society which is suffering while engaged
in a justified war.

The right of association and public protest

Experience of his own weakness both impels and encourages a man to
ally his forces with those of another. As the Bible puts it: brother helped
by brother is a fortress, friends are like the bar of a keep. Societies
which are formed within the state are said to be private, and rightly so
because their immediate purpose is the particular interest of their own
members. [*Rerum Novarum* 49]

There will be occasions when the law may rightly intervene against
private associations, as when some pursue policies which are contrary
to justice and the good of the state itself. However, great care must be
taken lest the right of citizens be emptied of content and unreasonable
regulations be made under the pretence of the public good.
[*Rerum Novarum* 51]

The right to conscientious objection to bearing arms

It seems right that laws make humane provisions for the case of those who, for reasons of conscience, refuse to bear arms, provided however that they agree to serve the human community in some other way. Those who devote themselves to the military service of their country should regard themselves as the agents of security and freedom of peoples, making a genuine contribution to the establishment of peace.
[*Gaudium et Spes* 79]

7. The right to revolt against an unjust ruler

The authority of the state comes to the rulers through the people, and not directly from God, and its purpose is the common good. Hence if the ruler governs for his own private good or that of any one section, or group of sections, of society and not for all – to the point where the stability and coherence of the social order and state is threatened – then there must be open to the citizens the right, in principle, to remove him by force. The conditions for taking this step of revolt are very exacting. It is, of course, not for the Church to encourage, still less initiate, such action and she must always caution in favour of peace; but since the political order has its own autonomy under the natural law and it is for the laity to direct that order, then it is up to their properly informed consciences to decide when it is necessary. Their pastors can counsel them but the decision is not theirs to make.

Implicit, then, in the nature of the political order, the right to revolt was specifically developed by theologians, notably by St Thomas Aquinas, and has been accepted by tradition. Francisco Suarez [1548– 1617] was very strict in determining when the right could be invoked: it amounted to an overthrow by constitutional means in a stable state. As a theorist it was his duty to be as rigorous as possible, lest he be seen in any way to countenance reckless insurrection, but it cannot therefore be assumed that in a non-constitutional state, a tyranny, the right no longer exists. So great are the uncertainties, permutations and possibilities in such a situation that it is not possible to schematise them all theoretically. However, the conditions for a just war have relevance here, especially the question of proportionality – weighing the possibilities of less suffering being imposed on the citizens by revolution, than by tolerating the tyrant. This principle can be invoked when different courses of action each seem to have consequences for which one would rather not have moral responsibility; but when there is no alternative but to make a choice, the choice can be made according to conscience, provided always that that choice does not involve committing objective evil.

> A tyrannical government is not just, because it is directed not to the common good but to the private good of the ruler. Consequently there is no sedition in disturbing a government of this kind, unless indeed the tyrant's rule be disturbed so inordinately that his subjects suffer greater harm from the consequent disturbance than the tyrant's government. It is the tyrant rather that is guilty, since he encourages discord and sedition. [*Summa Theologica* IIa IIae Q 42 Art 2 ad 3]

> The Church's Magisterium admits the recourse to armed struggle as a last resort to put an end to an obvious and prolonged tyranny which is gravely damaging to the fundamental rights of individuals and the common good. [*Libertatis Conscientia* 79]

> But those who discredit the path of reform and favour the myth of revolution not only foster the illusion that the abolition of an evil situation is in itself sufficient to create a more human society; they also encourage the setting up of totalitarian regimes. The fight against injustice is meaningless unless it is waged with a view to establishing a new social and political order in conformity with the demands of justice. [*Libertatis Conscientia* 78]

8. The relationship between Church and State

Christ made it plain that his kingdom was not of this world, and he resisted any attempt to force on him any direct political or social role – 'Render to Caesar the things that are Caesar's, and to God the things that are God's' was his advice. There is a tension here, as the testimony of the early martyrs shows; but there is also a harmony, seen in the fact that the early Christians went about doing good. The indirect influence of the Church on the secular world was positive and ultimately irresistible. It was the sheer goodness of the Christian way of life, its practical charity to all, the example of faithful service of all that was good in secular life, and the moral courage and probity that it instilled that eventually enabled Christianity to rebuild the foundations of society, and receive the grateful approval of Rome for so doing.

However, the tension remained. In the fifth century, Pope Gelasius pointed out to the Eastern Emperor that God had established two powers on earth: that of the secular power for the governance of the state, and that of ordained ministry for the care of the Church. Each was independent and autonomous, under the law of God, in its own sphere. Although, since the Church dealt with the things of God she ultimately had the precedence, this did not mean that she could directly interfere in state affairs, nor did it mean that in those aspects of her life which touched on the secular she did not have to obey the state. By the same token, the State could not presume to decide on theological and ecclesiological issues.

In Western Europe c 500 – 1100 waves of invasions were followed by the absorption of the invaders into the emerging European order, as they were baptised and settled. The Church civilised as she Christianised the new peoples, and her strong social organisation from the grass roots through parish, monastery, diocese and archdiocese throughout the Western world, gave her a cultural hegemony and a role of leadership. The Church did not seek this role, but in charity she could not refuse to undertake it[2]. For some eight hundred years Church and State were one, with the Church having the more effective and sophisticated organisation, and personnel throughout Europe. Her Bishops and Popes often had more experience and proven competence in government than the average feudal lord or Emperor, and her parishes were the centres of ordered local life. As a result she was the first of the 'estates' or social orders.

It caused her problems. Most notably she was an essential prop of what civilised social order had emerged by the twelfth century. Theological dissenters therefore not only undermined the Church's teaching and discipline, but they undermined society too, because it was the Church which held society together, providing the glue that sustained the social fabric. To peoples who had only just emerged from centuries of social chaos and who did not like the idea of slipping back into it, an attack on the Church was an attack on the foundations of society.

The needs of the situation had given her a role which was not hers: she was elected to lead Europe at a time when there was no other authority to do so. Inevitably then, the state expected her co-operation in the suppression of heresy and she was so much a part of the structure of things that she thought this was her duty too. The result was that for hundreds of years the Gelasian theory was obscured, though not repudiated. Then, after the Protestant reformation, the need to obtain the co-operation of the Catholic monarchs for the evangelisation of the new worlds being discovered, and to secure the faith in Europe from its enemies, put the Church and the Papacy in the thrall of those monarchs.

Only with the French Revolution was their stranglehold on the Church broken, but the revolution and its aftermath threatened her with a new enthralment. Since the Revolution was ostensibly democratic, but always potentially totalitarian and unstable, most European democracies up to the end of the second world war bore these marks. The Church then did not wholeheartedly accept such government in its modern form, despite her conviction that authority came to the ruler through the people. The people's government, like any other form, had to operate within the limits of the natural and revealed moral law. Not until the 1940s did political developments and the experience of the international Church throughout the world convince it that modern democracy could do that.

Since the excessive influence of Catholic states on Papal conclaves and national Churches had eventually been eliminated from the early twentieth century, the Gelasian theory of the relationship between State and Church could also be reaffirmed authoritatively and applied effectively. So it was that the second Vatican Council could confidently reaffirm both the Church's ancient belief in popular sovereignty and her own freedom in dealing with the political authorities, they respecting its autonomy and the Church respecting that of the secular order. Thus she could teach her children accordingly.

The Gelasian theory and popular sovereignty reaffirmed

The political community and the public authority are based on human nature and so belong to an order established by God; nevertheless, the choice of political regimes and the appointment of rulers are left to the free decision of the citizens. [*Gaudium et Spes* 74]

The Church, by reason of her role and competence, is not identified in any way with the political community nor bound to any political system. She is at once a sign and a safeguard of the transcendent character of the human person. [*Gaudium et Spes* 76]

The Church and the political community in their own fields are autonomous and independent from each other. Yet both are concerned with the personal and social vocation of the same men. The more that both foster healthier co-operation, the more effective will their service be exercised for the good of all. [*Gaudium et Spes* 76]

At all times and in all places the Church should have true freedom to preach the faith, to teach her social doctrine, to pass moral judgement on matters which concern the public order when the fundamental rights of the person or the salvation of souls requires it. She should make use of all the means which accord with the Gospel, and which correspond with the common good, with due regard to the circumstances, time and place. [*Gaudium et Spes* 76]

The clergy to avoid partisan politics

Pastors must be concerned with unity. So they will divest themselves of every partisan ideology that might condition their criteria and attitudes. Then they will be able to evangelise the political sphere without any infusion of partisanship or ideologisation. [*Puebla: evangelisation at present and in the future of Latin America*, Third General Council of Latin American Bishops, London 1980, p 110]

You are servants of the People of God, servants of Christ's love for men, a love that is not partisan, that excludes no one, although it is addressed preferably to the poorest. You are priests and religious, you are not social or political leaders or officials of a temporal power. Let us not be under the illusion that we are serving the Gospel if we dilute our

charism through an exaggerated interest in temporal problems.
[Address of John Paul II to priests and religious at Guadalupe, 27.1.79,
Puebla: Pilgrimage of Faith, Boston 1979, p 71]

Human development should not obscure the essential significance the
Church attributes to evangelisation and the Gospel. The priest should
inspire lay Catholics; in the promotion of justice, theirs is the more
demanding role. Tasks proper to each should not be confused. The
promotion of justice should be according to directives of the local
hierarchy.   [Letter of the Cardinal Secretary of State to Fr. Arrupe, 2nd
May 1975, *Documents of the 31st and 32nd General Congregations of
the Society of Jesus*, St Louis 1977, p 545f]

9. Justified war

There is a strong strain of pacifism in the Catholic tradition because of
the teaching and example of Christ, though it has always been a counsel
of perfection not a precept. We can infer from Christ's actions and
teaching as a whole, rather than from his free acceptance of his own
fate in offering no resistance to his passion and death, that he did not
rule out the use of force in defence of the good. His action in driving
out the of the temple the buyers and sellers who were defiling it, and
his own sharp questioning of the temple guard who struck him,
concerning the justification for so doing, are cases in point. His
readiness to use the good example of centurions on two occasions
would suggest that a military career was not incompatible with his
teaching. It is also notable that when soldiers came to St John the
Baptist asking what they must do to be saved, they were not told to
abandon their profession.

Many of the Fathers of the Church were unwilling to accept that it
was possible to reconcile soldiering and Christianity, but, by the time
the Church came out of the shadows towards the end of the second
century, it is obvious that many were doing so. In the time of the
Emperor Marcus Aurelius, the contribution of the Christians in the
Legio Fulminata [the 'Thundering Legion'] to the Roman cause was
commemorated on a column erected in Rome. Meanwhile the number

of soldiers who were martyred in every Province of the Empire during the persecutions of the third and early fourth century shows that there were many Christians serving willingly in the legions, and whose conflict with Rome was not over pacifism but the refusal to worship any other God but Jesus Christ.

When Rome accepted that Christianity was not its enemy, tolerating and indeed welcoming its presence, the question of pacifism came up in another form. Christians in government or the military had to bear some responsibility in defence of the State, and it was in this context that St Augustine developed the theory of the justified use of violence. It is better called a theory of justified war, rather than baldly 'Just war theory', because the latter has about it an absolute ring, as if it were a good in itself, whereas no Christian can see war as anything but an evil – a necessary evil in an imperfect world, but an evil nonetheless. Augustine's teaching was the basis of St Thomas Aquinas' own, but was not taken up officially into the Church's teaching until the *Catechism of the Catholic Church* [1996]. Before that it had been common and accepted teaching in practice only.

The traditional teaching on the just war

In order for a war to be just, three things are necessary. Firstly, the authority of the sovereign. It is not the business of the private individual to declare war. The care of the common weal is committed to those in authority. Secondly, a just cause is required. A just war avenges wrongs or restores what has been seized unjustly. Thirdly, the belligerents should have a right intention – the advancement of good or the avoidance of evil; not for motives or aggrandisement or cruelty, but of securing peace or punishing evildoers. [*Summa Theologica* IIa IIae Q 40 Art 1]

The modern teaching; weapons of mass destruction; deterrence

The question of proportionality – weighing the evil that is being opposed against the evil that waging war will bring – has always posed problems, which have increased vastly as modern weapons have grown more sophisticated. The problem has become more acute with the development of nuclear, bacteriological and chemical weapons, and the countermeasures of deterrence – the possession of these armaments on the grounds that it was necessary to have them to deter aggressors. Some thought that such a doctrine was indefensible and that Christians should be forbidden in any way to co-operate in the manufacture, transport or preparation for the hypothetical use of such weapons of deterrence. This would of course have put the Church in direct conflict with the State on a matter which was ultimately in the latter's competence.

The Church must advise on the moral issues, but she may not usurp the State's authority. Since it could be reasonably claimed that there was a case for deterrence, as a temporary expedient looking to eventual disarmament, it had to be accepted.

> Every act of war aimed indiscriminately at the destruction of entire cities or extensive areas along with their population is a crime against God and man himself. It merits unequivocal condemnation.
> [*Gaudium et Spes* 80]

> In current conditions, deterrence, based on balance, certainly not as an end in itself but as a step on the way to progressive disarmament, may still be judged morally acceptable. Nonetheless to ensure peace, it is indispensable not to be satisfied with the minimum, which is always susceptible to the real danger of explosion.
> [*The Challenge of Peace,* US Bishops' Pastoral on War and Peace in a Nuclear Age, London 1983, para 173, quoting John Paul II]

The modern teaching overall summarised

The conditions for legitimate defence by military force require rigorous consideration.

At one and the same time:

− the damage inflicted by the aggressor on the nation or community of nations must be lasting, grave and certain;
− all other means of putting an end to it must have been shown to be impractical or ineffective;
− there must be serious prospects of success;

– the use of arms must not produce evils and disorders graver than the evil to be eliminated. The power of modern means of destruction weighs very heavily in evaluating this condition.

The evaluation of these conditions for moral legitimacy belongs to the prudential judgement of those who have responsibility for the common good.

The Church and human reason both assert the permanent validity of the moral law during armed combat. The mere fact that war has regrettably broken out does not mean that everything becomes licit between the warring parties. Non-combatants, wounded soldiers and prisoners must be treated humanely. Actions deliberately contrary to the law of nations and its universal principles are crimes as are the orders that command them. Blind obedience does not excuse those who carry them out. Thus the extermination of a people, nation or ethnic minority must be condemned.

[*Catechism of the Catholic Church*, London 1996, 2309–2313]

10. International relations

The relationship between states and heads of states are, like those between individuals, the subject of reciprocal rights and duties based on truth, justice and freedom according to the needs of humanity. There are great differences between states in terms of population and resources, stages of development and power, but the rights of the less powerful must be respected and conflicts between states should be settled by negotiation not force of arms. The complexity of modern life means that some international authority is needed with the power, the organisation and means adequate to securing the international common good. This must be built up on the principle of subsidiarity, so that it has the full co-operation of individual states. The United Nations Organisation has done much to these ends, and the hope is that it may be able to fulfil the expectations resting on it more fully.

Relations between states

Nations are the subject of reciprocal rights and duties. Their relationships therefore must be harmonised in accordance with the dictates of truth, justice, willing co-operation and freedom. The same law that governs the life and conduct of individuals must also regulate the relations of political communities with one another. [*Pacem in Terris* 80]

Truth calls for the elimination of every trace of racial discrimination; all states are by their nature equal in dignity, each has the right to exist, to develop and possess the necessary means to and accept the primary responsibility for its own development. Relations between states must be related by justice, the recognition of mutual rights and respective duties. States are duty-bound to safeguard such rights effectively and avoid any action that would violate them. [*Pacem in Terris* 86–92]

There sometimes is a clash of interests between states. They must be settled by a mutual assessment of the arguments and feelings of both sides, an objective investigation of the situation and a reconciliation of opposing views. [*Pacem in Terris* 93]

An international authority is needed to secure the international common good

Each country's social progress, order, security and peace are necessarily linked with those of every other country. No state can fittingly pursue its own interests in isolation from the rest, nor develop itself as it should. There will always be an imperative need to promote in sufficient measure the universal common good. [*Pacem in Terris* 131–2]

The universal common good presents us with problems which cannot be solved except by a public authority with power, organisation and means co-extensive with these problems. The moral order demands some general form of political authority. The principle of subsidiarity must apply. It is no part of the duty of universal authority to limit the sphere of action of the authority of individual states. The essential purpose is to create conditions in which the authorities of each nation can fulfil its duties with greater security. [*Pacem in Terris* 137– 141]

It is our earnest wish that the United Nations Organisation may be able progressively to adapt its structure and methods to the magnitude and nobility of its tasks. [*Pacem in Terris* 145]

Chapter Three
Ethics and Economic Society

1. Introduction

Economic society develops as man applies himself to the task of earning a living and improving his material conditions of existence by agriculture, industry, commerce, trade, in the professions and arts and in other occupations. The structures and mechanisms of economic society must respect the dignity of the man who works, and his spiritual, moral and intellectual needs as well as his material needs. He must have freedom to choose his work, to prosper at it and to own property. Unless he has these freedoms all other freedoms are at risk from his economic masters. It is the task of the state to ensure economic freedom and to see that that freedom is not abused, but that, through it, all may have access to the means of a decent livelihood. To these ends it can regulate the ownership and use of private property for the common good, but may not use these powers to undermine the institution itself.

2. The purpose of the economy

Meeting human need

The purpose of the economic and social organism is to provide its members and their families with all the goods which the resources of nature and of industry, with the social organisation of economic life, can procure for them. And, as is made clear in *Quadragesimo Anno*, these goods ought to be plentiful enough to satisfy all reasonable needs and to raise them to that level of comfort which, if used wisely, is far from being an obstacle to virtue but rather a valuable help to it.
[Pius XII to the President of the *Semaines Sociales*, 7 July 1952, quoted in J-Y Calvez and J. Perrin, *The Church and Social Justice*, London 1961, p 175]

The ultimate and basic purpose of economic production does not merely consist in the increase of goods produced, nor in profit nor in prestige; it is directed to the service of man, that is of man in his totality, taking into account his material needs and the requirements of his intellectual, moral, spiritual and religious life. Economic activity is to be carried out according to its own methods and laws, within the limits of the moral order, so that God's design for mankind may be fulfilled.
[*Gaudium et Spes* 64]

The dangers of consumerism

We find ourselves up against a super-development which consists in an excessive availability of every kind of goods for certain groups which easily makes people slaves of possessions with no other horizon than the multiplication of or continual replacement of things already owned with others still better. This is the civilisation of consumption or consumerism. [*Sollicitudo Rei Socialis* 28]

In the earlier stages of development, man always lived under the weight of necessity. His needs were few. The problem today is of consumerism. It is not wrong to want to live better. What is wrong is a style of life which wants more in order to spend life in enjoyment as an end in itself. In consumerism, people are ensnared in a web of false and superficial gratification rather than being helped to experience their personhood in an authentic way. [*Centesimus Annus* 36, 41]

3. Labour

If the end of the economy is to satisfy the human need for the goods required for decent existence, then the essential means to that end is labour. God gave the earth to all for their sustenance, but the earth does not yield its fruits and other products on a scale which satisfies their human needs without human effort. It is through work, the use of intelligence, and freedom in developing the world, that man does this. Initially, man had no capital or complex tools, only the land and his capacity for work. All property originated in labour, and that is why labour has priority over property, and over capital.

Work has a spiritual as well as an economic significance. It is man, made in God's image, who works and so shares in the creative activity of his maker, who is depicted in the scriptures as working in the creation of his world. That work has been given a new dignity by the example of God the Son made man, who spent most of his life on earth working with his hands for a living. Some kinds of labour were respected in the classical world: the craftsman could be honoured, as could the free peasant toiling on his own land; but generally manual work, especially the humbler tasks, was despised, and it was seen as coarsening man in body and soul. Christ's example gave a different emphasis. All honest work is ennobled in that it is man, made in God's image and likeness, who does it. The *subject* of work is more important than the work done or the *object* achieved by it.

There is also a punitive side to work. That man should earn his living by hard toil was one of the punishments which God visited on man because of sin. But man can also find great satisfaction in his work, and when he cannot he can unite his hardships to those of Christ the Worker. However, the materialistic economism of the liberal capitalist Industrial Revolution from the eighteenth century, saw work and the worker as on a par with the inanimate commodities – as things, factors of production rather than persons. The workers reacted through forming their trades unions, and society eventually saw social legislation as necessary to curb the worst excesses of the crueller employers. Where the spirit of liberal capitalism remains such watchfulness is still needed.

Marx saw the excesses of liberal capitalism as justification for, and indeed making scientifically predictable and inevitable, the class war and the destruction of the state. This, he believed, would lead to the dictatorship of the proletariat en route to the socialist paradise in which there would be no private ownership of productive goods. But the Church rejected this on the grounds that it was only through private initiative that the increase in wealth, which would satisfy the needs of the poor, could be created. She also rejected that labour and capital are opposed. All capital originated in labour, in the order of being, therefore the two cannot be totally opposed. On the contrary, they should co-operate; while each should look after the interests it represents, it must be within such a co-operative framework.

Properly considered, the employer and the employed are both workers on the same work bench, with different functions, but united by their common purpose of efficient production to meet the needs of their fellow citizens. It is true that the tensions induced by the defects of the liberal capitalist tradition, make it difficult for this ideal to be put into effect, but there are enough good employers, and workers ready to respond to them, to demonstrate that the Church's instinct here is sound.

Priority of labour, by hand and brain

We recall a principle that has always been taught by the Church. The priority of labour over capital. This principle directly concerns the process of production. In this process labour is always the primary, efficient cause, while capital, the whole collection of the means of production, remains a mere instrument or instrumental cause. [*Laborem Exercens* 12]

The ancient world saw the work of muscles and hands as unworthy of free men and was therefore given to slaves. The Old Testament, and Christianity's gospel of work, show that the basis of determining the value of human work is not primarily the kind of work done but the fact that the one doing it is a person. The sources of the dignity of work are to be sought primarily in the subjective dimension not the objective. [*Laborem Exercens* 6]

In our time the role of human work is becoming increasingly important as the productive factor. Moreover, it is becoming clearer how a person's work is inter-related with the work of others, sharing a community of work. Many goods require the co-operation of many people. Organising such a productive effort, planning, making sure it corresponds to demand and taking necessary risks are all a source of wealth in today's society. The role of disciplined and creative human work, and, as an essential part of that work, entrepreneurial ability, becomes increasingly evident and decisive. [*Centesimus Annus* 31, 32]

The spiritual significance of work

In the Book of Genesis, the creation activity itself is presented as work done by God during six days. Genesis shows what the dignity of work consists of: man ought to imitate God his Creator in working. [*Laborem Exercens* 25]

The truth that, by work, man participates in the activity of God himself is given particular prominence by Jesus Christ the carpenter. Jesus fulfilled the gospel of work because he who proclaimed it was a man of work, a craftsman like Joseph of Nazareth. [*Laborem Exercens* 26]

There is another essential aspect of human work, that is profoundly imbued with the spirituality based on the Gospel: the curse of toil that sin brought with it. *Cursed is the ground because of you; in toil you shall eat of it all the days of your life*. The Christian finds in human work a small part of the cross of Christ, and accepts it in the same spirit of redemption in which Christ accepted his cross for us. [*Laborem Exercens* 27]

The objective and subjective aspects of work

Work understood as a 'transitive activity', that is to say beginning in the human subject and directed towards an external object, presupposes a specific dominion by man over the earth. This throws light on human work. Thus there emerges the meaning of work in the objective sense – [for example] agriculture and industry, the toil of human hands aided by machinery. [*Laborem Exercens* 4, 5]

Man has to subdue the earth because as an image of God he is a person, a subjective being capable of deciding about himself and with a tendency to self-realisation. Human work has a value all of its own; the one who carries it out is a person, a conscious and free subject who decides about himself. [*Laborem Exercens* 6]

Materialistic economism and Marxism

Entrepreneurs tried to establish the lowest possible wages and there were other elements of exploitation. This found expression in the conflict

between liberalism, the ideology of capitalism, and Marxism.
[*Laborem Exercens* 11]

Capital was set in opposition to labour, considering labour only
according to its economic purpose: the materialistic error of economism.
[*Laborem Exercens* 13]

Marxism, the ideology of scientific socialism as the spokesman of the
working class, transformed the conflict between labour and capital into
a systematic class struggle to eliminate class injustices and the
collectivisation of the means of production. [*Laborem Exercens* 11]

The legitimate title to ownership of the means of production lies in the service of labour

Property is acquired first of all through work in order that it may serve
work. This concerns in a special way the ownership of the means of
production. The only legitimate title to their possession – whether in the
form of private ownership or in the form of public or collective ownership
is that they should serve labour and thus, by serving labour, they should
make possible the achievement of the first principle of this order – namely
the universal destination of created goods. [*Laborem Exercens* 14]

4. Property

Property refers to the ownership of material things: land, houses,
productive goods, capital, natural resources, plant and machinery;
luxury goods, precious stones and metals and works of art. It also
includes intellectual property, products of creative ability protected
by law. The right to own private property was recognised by both the
Old Testament and the New, and it was seen as a moral good, rather
than as a concession to human weakness. In *Genesis*, God gave man a
limited dominion over the earth and all that is in it, teaching that its
natural resources, the plants, were all there for his service. The
limitations of the dominion concern the use of these things: they must
be used properly, with respect for God's creation. The environment

must be preserved, resources must not be used wastefully, animals must not be abused but treated with respect as God's creatures. Animals however are not persons, as they do not have a human intelligence and free will. Moral responsibility cannot be expected of them, so they cannot have rights and duties. We have a duty to them but they cannot have a duty to us.

God gave the world to all men in common, so that they might use its gifts for their benefit, and this universal destination of created goods gives us a proper perspective on private ownership: it is a good insofar as it helps mankind to realise the universal purpose for which the goods of the world were created. Reflecting on the scriptures and human experience, the Church has seen that it is impossible for all men to share goods in common throughout the world; such an ideal cannot be realised because there is no authority to guarantee that it would work justly, and the logistics of it would be impossible, with everyone having the right to possess what they wanted at whim, and with no regard for the need of others.

However, it is possible for national states and other communities to make just laws governing private property. We can find an authority for doing so in Scripture, where there is the example of God's actions when he chose a people to serve him: he gave each family the right to private property, a piece of land for their support; and he protected this by his Law (in the Seventh and Tenth Commandments). The New Testament has confirmed this (cf *Matthew* 19:18), as has the common experience of mankind. Unlike slavery and divorce, private property is not considered in the Scriptures to be an evil to be tolerated until humanity can be brought to a better understanding. Private property is actually a positive moral good, if honestly gained and properly used.

At the same time we must keep in mind that the scriptures tell us in plain and unmistakable terms that the possession of wealth, and especially great wealth, is very dangerous to man's spiritual well-being. Being possessed of it, man feels so secure, and has so much power, that he tends to forget he is a contingent being; he begins to consider himself free from any moral restraint, that he can defy God and his law with impunity. The Church must then preach the danger of the love of riches. At the same time, she recognises that a decent standard of material existence is necessary for every man if he is to lead a life worthy of his human dignity. She should encourage those who are concerned with the production of wealth to be efficient in their task. She must also seek to make sure that the State, which has care of the common good, ensures that the resultant goods are in fact made to serve the needs of all.

The right to private ownership of productive goods is a natural right

More and more people, through insurance and social security, face the future with the sort of confidence that formerly came from property. Today people are aiming at proficiency in their trade or profession; and this is as it should be: they think more highly of it than of an income which derives from capital. Work is the expression of human personality; external goods are merely instrumental. [*Mater et Magistra* 105–107]

The right of private ownership of goods, including productive goods, has permanent validity. It is part of the natural order, which teaches that the individual is prior to society and society must be ordered to the good of the individual. It would be quite useless to insist on free personal initiative in the economic field while withdrawing the means indispensable to it. History testifies that in political regimes which do not recognise rights to private ownership, freedom is suppressed or stifled. [*Mater et Magistra* 109]

Property contributes to the expression of personality, furnishes one an occasion to exercise his function in society and is necessary for the autonomy of the person and the family and should be regarded as an extension of human freedom. It adds incentives for carrying out one's function and duty; it constitutes one of the civil liberties. [*Gaudium et Spes* 71]

The only legitimate title to the ownership of the means of production is that they serve labour thus achieving the universal purpose of created things. [*Laborem Exercens* 14]

The universal purpose of created goods and its implications for the state

God intended the earth with everything contained in it for the use of all human beings and peoples. Thus, under guidance of justice, together with charity, created goods should be in abundance for all in an equitable manner. Whatever the forms of property may be, attention must always be paid to this universal distribution of goods. [*Gaudium et Spes* 69]

The social character of ownership implies that men must consider in this matter not only their own interests but also the common good. Therefore public authority can determine more accurately what is permitted and not permitted to owners in the use of their property. Moreover, God has left the limits of private possessions to be fixed by the industry of men and the institutions of peoples. The State must not discharge its duty arbitrarily, however. The natural right to property and inheritance is a right which the State cannot take away.
[*Quadragesimo Anno* 49]

The state may own productive goods and expropriate private property with compensation, where the common good requires it

For certain kinds of property, it is rightly contended, ought to be reserved to the State since they carry with them a dominating power so great that they cannot without danger be entrusted to private individuals.
[*Quadragesimo Anno* 114]

The lawfulness of private ownership is not opposed to forms of public ownership. Transfer of goods to public ownership must be undertaken by competent authority in accordance with the common good and accompanied by adequate compensation. [*Gaudium et Spes* 71]

In several economically retarded areas there exist rural estates which are slightly cultivated or not cultivated at all for the sake of profit, while the majority of people have no land. When the common good calls for expropriation, compensation must be made according to equity.
[*Gaudium et Spes* 71]

5. Capital and capitalism

Capital and financial resources are a particular form of private property and are governed by the same ethical principles in their use. The word 'capital' in itself has no connotations of morality or immorality. Capital is what we possess when, out of our income, we have paid our bills and have something left over. If we have savings, we have capital. So it is a form of money, money which is a unit of account (giving us a standard by which we can measure wealth), a means of exchange (the money we hand over when we buy something), and a store of value (which we can keep because we do not have to spend it until we decide that there is something we want to spend it on). One thing we can spend it on, if we have enough spare capital, is productive goods. We can invest it and make our investment productive.

This is how the word 'capital' came to be applied to one form of expenditure in particular: investment to make more money. It did so because, when the emerging civilisation of the central and late middle ages [c. 1000 to 1500 AD], developed a commercial and industrial sector[3], production of goods was initially based on craft guild methods. In the first stages, the craftsman bought his own materials, owned his own tools and his own workshop and marketed his own product, employing a few apprentices and perhaps qualified craftsmen or 'journeymen' who worked for wages. This was enough to meet demand for the product in a small local market. When demand became national or even international, these methods of production were not enough. More money had to be invested in raw materials (often brought from a distance), in new machines and methods and bigger workshops. Few craftsmen had the ability or the opportunity to finance and organise on this larger scale. In consequence, whilst the crafts still flourished into the eighteenth and nineteenth century, a small number of men who had the money to invest and the ability to organise production began to dominate some sectors.

These were 'capitalists' and many of them were as ruthless in pursuit of gain as were the later capitalists of the industrial revolution. They could not and did not dominate the whole of society, however, and so they could not impose their standards on everyone – nor did Christian ethics encourage it. They were entitled to their wealth if they had earned it honestly, though there were still limits on how they could use or abuse it.

It was the 'Enlightenment'[4] in the eighteenth century which freed the capitalist from moral restraint. 'Laissez faire', 'let them get on with it', was the cry. The market was a moral force; all would be well if the capitalist were freed from moral restraints. The invisible hand of the economy would bring justice through selfishness. This principle revolutionised economics and economic organisation; it also tore both from links with objective morality. The Judaeo-Christian tradition of objective moral law knew that defrauding the labourer of his just rewards was a sin crying out to heaven for vengeance. Now the Enlightenment canonised the selfishness of the rich. The labourer had helped to create wealth beyond previous imagining, and was rewarded with whatever pittance his master offered him, according to the law of supply and demand in a market hopelessly tilted in favour of the master. An increasingly Godless age found in Marx an atheist prophet against this evil. His cure was worse than the disease, as experience would show; but the resultant sufferings imposed on man by real socialism are to be laid at the door of those who produced so violent a reaction in Marx and Engels – the materialistic economism of the liberal capitalists[5].

The capitalism in the period after 1780 in Britain (and subsequently in Europe and North America) which led to the abuses which angered Marx among others, was *industrial* capitalism – the application of machinery to the production of goods for the supply of mass markets. But in the early part of the twentieth century the capitalist world was rocked once again by the excesses of another form of capitalism – financial capitalism – whose madness lead to the 'Great Crash', the collapse of the New York stock market on 24th October 1929. The economic boom in the USA in the 1920s had led to the illusion that share prices on the stock market would always rise, and that if people bought stocks and shares they could always sell them at a higher price later. People who before would never have thought of investing in stocks and shares began to do so with ever greater recklessness, encouraged by experts, economists, businessmen, financial journalists, bankers, stockbrokers and the rest who believed that the boom would never end. But end it did, and then the selling started and the dream collapsed. It was a telling lesson in the dangers of reckless financial speculation and a get-rich-quick mentality. The effects upon the international economy were appalling; ironically it was only with the necessity of re-arming as the second World War approached that the capitalist economies started to revive fully.

But lessons were learned; national, social and economic policies changed slowly as war approached and then swiftly from 1945. The background was the recovery of the international economy from the early 1950s as the revival of international trade fuelled the greatest period of economic expansion ever known. The developed economies began to take full employment and the affluent society for granted. All this faded somewhat in the late 1970s, but did not collapse. More recently, in the 1990s, we have been reminded what a delicate mechanism the international economy is, as so-called 'tiger' economies have faltered and reckless speculation has threatened disaster again.

But capitalism has shown that it is a survivor: its liberal excesses have been checked by law, by changing conventions, by the organised forces of labour which wanted justice but within the existing system, and by those of the middle and upper classes who were prepared to accept the movement for social, political and economic reform. Yet it leaves the economic system of the West still tainted by the illusions of liberal capitalism – that profit-makers should be free of all restraint in the pursuit of their aim, and that the market should be allowed absolute freedom. Furthermore, in such a system, it is those countries whose political, economic and social structures are weakest that suffer the most.

Moral defects of Liberal capitalist industrialisation after 1780

The coming of new industrial growth has brought immense wealth for a small number and deepest poverty for the multitude. The people at the bottom of the social scale for the most part are in a condition of undeserved misery. Working men are now left isolated and helpless, betrayed to the inhumanity of employers and the unbridled greed of competitors. [Rerum Novarum 1, 2]

The first task is to save the wretched workers from the brutality of those who make of human beings mere instruments for the unrestrained acquisition of wealth. [*Rerum Novarum* 43]

We are witnessing a renewal of the liberal ideology. Certainly personal initiative must be maintained but at the very root of philosophical liberalism is an erroneous affirmation of the autonomy of the individual in his activity, his motivation and the exercise of his liberty. Liberal ideology calls for careful discernment. [*Octogesima Adveniens* 35]

Morally responsible capitalism can meet the needs of the poor

The socialists argue that the remedy for this evil [liberal capitalism] is the abolition of private property. But if this were done all incentive for individuals to exercise their ingenuity and skill would be removed and the very founts of wealth would dry up. The conclusion is inescapable. All who set out to improve the conditions of the masses must start from the fundamental principle that private possessions remain inviolate. [*Rerum Novarum* 3, 13]

With all his energy Leo XIII sought to adjust this economic system according to the norms of right order: hence it is evident that it is not to be condemned in itself. It is not of its nature vicious. But it does violate right order when capital hires workers according to its own will and advantage, scorning the human dignity of the workers, the social character of economic activity and the common good. [*Quadragesimo Anno* 101]

6. Capitalism and the market: Marxism and the failure of the command economy

The capitalist produces goods to sell at a profit in the market place, and the resulting economic pattern throughout society produces a market economy; that is an economy which aims, not at producing just enough to allow the producers to live at subsistence level for themselves, but goods which they can take to market. This process increases the wealth of the total community by expanding its economic activity. In a pre-market economy there are financial resources – money, or precious metals and stones which can be used or turned into money – lying idle. There are also other unused resources, men and women who have no paid work to do, land under-used, minerals and other resources not developed.

When traders make their goods and services available in the local market, people buy them if the price is right; the vendor makes a profit, the buyer has something he needed or wanted; and if they are capital goods, he increases his productivity. The process benefits the work-force because it protects their jobs as they make more such goods for sale. If there is a proper framework of just laws which encourage and support this pattern, and which secure the common good, then the system works for the benefit of all. It is necessary, for example, to protect the environment and to make sure that the parties to the process are not cheated and do not exploit others by some form of monopoly or other restraint of trade. If all these conditions are met then the economy is a truly healthy economy, because its purpose – meeting human need – is fulfilled in justice and freedom. Capital is then invested in the expanding sectors which are 'booming' because they are meeting people's needs, and their expansion provides useful employment. Such is the model which enables man to combine economic freedom with the effective service of the whole community, and to do so within the complex industrial economies which are necessary to develop the world's resources adequately for man's needs. Of course the model has never been perfectly realised, human affairs being what they are; but it gives a practical standard at which to aim.

Unfortunately, not all human needs can be brought to market; the market will only supply needs if they are backed up by the cash to buy. The market is a world in which exchange at equal cash value is the norm. The poor, unemployed or under-employed, the old and the sick too often do not have the cash necessary to come to market, and it is the first obligation of an economy to see that their needs are met. The dependency on the State of those able to work must be discouraged, but there are some who are incapable of supporting themselves entirely or even partially by work, and these people are a charge justifiably to be borne by the community.

The Marxist reaction to the evils of industrial capitalism – the rejection of the private ownership of productive goods – meant the end of the market as the core of economic life in Marxist-controlled countries. Markets always existed in some sectors, however, because they could not be done without entirely; but they did not dominate the economy. This meant that there was no way that consumer need could dictate the pattern of prices and investment as happened in the market economy; all these had to be determined by the planners at the centre. Hence the 'command' as opposed to the 'demand' or 'market' economy.

In war conditions, when all states have to make sure of war supplies, and the need for basic fairness in the distribution of consumer necessities and goods has an absolute priority, the free market has to be strictly controlled or suspended. Apart from these desperate conditions, the common experience of mankind and the facts of human nature are against a command economy. State 'fiat' or central planners cannot predict with efficiency and fairness what economic needs will have to be met, and how. The result is that things that are not needed are produced because the planner gets it wrong, and things that are needed are not produced, while production methods are so inefficient and profligate of manpower and resources, that costs are high. After little more than fifty years (1917–1967) it was apparent that the Marxist command economy was not working, and by 1989 it was gradually abandoned.

Capitalism and production for profit in the market

> Those who are engaged in producing goods, therefore, are not forbidden to increase their fortune in a just and lawful manner: for it is only fair that he who renders service to the community and makes it richer should also be made richer himself according to his position, provided that all these things are sought with due respect for the laws of God. [*Quadragesimo Anno* 136]

[Pius XII] agreed with Pius XI that capitalists and capitalism in general had a positive role to play in society. Profit should come from service rendered to the community. When this was realised, the concept of competition preserves its positive aspect, and one moreover it is necessary to emulate. [Pius XII, Radio Message of December 24th 1952 and an Address of June 22 1956, in R L Camp, *The Papal Ideology of Social Reform*, Leiden 1969, p 105]

The ability to foresee the needs of others, and the combinations of productive factors most adapted to satisfying those needs, constitutes another source of wealth in society. The role of disciplined and creative human work, initiative and responsibility becomes increasingly evident and decisive. [*Centesimus Annus* 32]

When a firm makes a profit, this means that productive factors have been properly employed and corresponding human needs have been satisfied. Profit is the regulator of business life, but human and moral factors must also be considered; they are at least equally important for the life of a business. [*Centesimus Annus* 35]

The market is not an autonomous moral force but a social mechanism, and as such is subject to the ultimate control of the State for the common good

Individualistic economic teaching held that economic life must be considered as free and independent of public authority, because the market would have a principle of self-direction which governs it more perfectly; but free competition, while justified and useful in certain limits, cannot curb itself. Social justice and social charity must govern it firmly and fully. [*Quadragesimo Anno* 88]

At the very root of philosophical liberalism is an erroneous affirmation of the autonomy of the individual in his activity, his motivation and the exercise of his liberty. The Liberal ideology calls for careful discernment. [*Octogesima adveniens* 35]

The market must be appropriately controlled by the forces of society and by the state so that the basic needs of the whole society are satisfied. [*Centesimus Annus* 35]

The market only responds to needs backed by purchasing power: fundamental needs must not go unsatisfied because of a lack of such power

> It would seem that the market is the most efficient instrument for responding to needs. But this is true only for needs endowed with purchasing power and many needs do not have that power. Needy people must be helped to enter the circle of exchange and to develop their skills in order to make the best use of their capacities and resources. Even prior to the logic of fair exchange of goods, there is something that is due to man because he is man. Inseparable from that something is the possibility to survive and at the same time make an active contribution to the common good. [*Centesimus Annus* 34]

Some moral problems of mature capitalism

The social problems of the nineteenth century were those of liberal industrial capitalism: failing to give to the wage earner and his family decent wages and conditions or a stake in the system. In the 1920s and 1930s it was the weaknesses of financial liberalism, in its banking and financial institutions that dominated the international economy, which failed the people. There has been an echo of this within the last decade with problems of ordering the international economy in an era of globalisation. Speculative international financial dealings threaten the stability of the international economy. More sophisticated international co-operation and mechanisms are needed to ensure that such markets work for the common good internationally and not against it.

In national economies the machinations which accompany major take-overs are so obscurely understood that, when wrong-doing is suspected and the law seeks to prosecute those concerned, it defies lawyers and accountants to discover who did what and when, and the case can collapse in consequence. Major insurance companies have been found to have been operating in an unacceptable manner, with their sales forces misleading and cheating their clients. Massive penalties have had to be imposed on them; even then the processing of claims has, in some cases, been so dilatory that it has caused further scandal.

Consumerism results in consumption for its own sake, which is morally debilitating, yet powerful advertising encourages it – things are preferred to people and material wealth is made the only measure of worth. At the same time, the assumption is made that choice is an absolute, and this warps the value system and produces social evils. Choice irrespective of the good or evil of what is chosen results in socially disruptive behaviour, such as drug taking, over-indulgence in alcohol, pornography, exploitative sex and the claiming of the 'right' to choose abortion. At some point society has to face up to these evils. Finally, there is a number of older problems with the market economy and capitalism that still demand attention: e.g. price fixing and all forms of dishonesty in the daily transaction of business.

> The easy gains which a market unrestricted by any law opens to everybody, attracts those who aim to make quick profits with the least expenditure of work, by raising or lowering prices by their uncontrolled business dealings according to their own caprice and greed. The laws passed to promote corporate business, while dividing and limiting the risk of business have given occasion to the most sordid license. [*Quadragesimo Anno* 132]

> Of itself an economic system does not possess criteria for correctly distinguishing new and higher forms of satisfying need from artificial new needs which hinder the formation of a mature personality. Thus a great deal of educational and cultural work is needed as well as the necessary intervention by public authorities. [*Centesimus Annus* 36]

> It is necessary to create lifestyles in which the quest for beauty, goodness and communion with others for the sake of common growth are the factors which determine consumer choices, savings and investment. [*Centesimus Annus* 36]

> Any form of taking or keeping the property of others is against the seventh commandment, as is deliberate retention of goods lent or objects lost; business fraud, forcing up prices or taking advantage of the ignorance or hardship of another. Also morally illicit are speculation in which one contrives to manipulate prices artificially and corruption in which one influences the judgement of those who must make decisions according to law. [*Catechism of the Catholic Church* 2409]

Promises must be kept and contracts strictly observed to the extent that the commitments made in them are morally just. All contracts must be agreed to and executed in good faith.
[*Catechism of the Catholic Church* 2410]

Capitalism after the failure of the Marxist economy. The only alternative?

It would appear that the free market is the most efficient instrument for utilising resources and effectively responding to needs.
[*Centesimus Annus* 34]

Should capitalism be the model to be proposed to countries searching for the path to true economic and civil progress?

If by capitalism is meant the positive role of business, the market, private property and responsibility for the means of production as well as free creativity in the economic sector, the answer is in the affirmative; though it would be more appropriate to speak of a business economy, market economy or simply free economy.

But if by capitalism is meant a system in which freedom in the economic sector is not circumscribed within a strong juridical framework which places it at the service of human freedom nor is seen as a particular aspect of freedom, the core of which is ethical and religious, then the reply is certainly negative. [*Centesimus Annus* 42]

As an alternative to the absolute predominance of capitalism and socialism is proposed a society of free work, of enterprise and participation. Such a society is not directed against the market but demands that the market be appropriately controlled by the forces of society and by the state so as to guarantee that the basic needs of the whole of society are recognised. [*Centesimus Annus* 35]

7. The capitalist enterprise, and its employees

The individual business enterprise – the firm or its equivalent – is the basic unit of the capitalist economy in all its branches (industry, commerce, trade, finance, services, mining, fishing and farming). The organisation of the enterprise is fundamentally hierarchical: the owner or managing director and his colleagues control the organisation and engage its middle management and those who work under it in their various capacities. Where the firm is smaller, or in the case of small-scale farming, the organisation is less complex, but the principle is the same: that ultimately one man, or one group of managers, controls the whole operation. This is necessary in order that decision making be prompt and accountable, and responsibility clear.

From the late eighteenth century, liberal capitalists used people in the pursuit of the maximum profit on their labour in such a manner as to call into doubt whether industrial capitalism could ever again be trusted to treat its employees humanely. The Marxists thought that it could not. The Church, in *Rerum Novarum,* said that capitalists could be trusted, given the right action by the Church, the State and the parties to the wage contract.

This is the way it evolved: in Western Europe and in America, where the liberal capitalist Industrial Revolution first began and where it first flourished, the trades unions and the working class generally were ready to work for a better deal with the capitalists, not to destroy them. Marx thought that he had a chance, during his residence in England 1849–81, to rouse the British workers, and the international labour movement, to behave as his theories said they should behave. However, they spectacularly failed to do so. His failure demonstrated what any serious objective examination of his theories reveals, that he had little understanding of real workers or the real world.

Nonetheless, some of Marx's insights – the alienation of the worker in particular – contained a strong element of truth. Liberal capitalism has been curbed through legislation, social and political pressures and countervailing forces, but its philosophy still dominates the wishes and will of modern capitalism. This is shown whenever it is given the freedom to do as it wishes without let or hindrance – in some areas of industry, commerce and finance in the first world, but much more graphically in the third world, where life is harder and government and public opinion is weaker, or more easily defied. There the alienation can be complete.

Central to the whole question of a worker's rights in industry is that of adequate wages. Work is a personal as well as a social obligation: its primary character is subjective, it is the work of a human being, arising out of the obligation to work for a living. Full-time work must then return to the workers, who meet their obligation to work honestly and well for their employers, a wage sufficient to support them and their families in a decent manner. In a free society and a market economy, the wage must ultimately depend on a free agreement between the employer and the employed, but society has an obligation to ensure that such agreements do provide a wage adequate for human needs. From here the means of giving the employee a greater sense of identity and fulfilment at work can be worked out – by making the workplace a true community, and by adapting the wage contract in some way, so that he can participate in the profits of the business.

Liberal capitalism and worker solidarity in the 19th century

In the last century there arose the worker, or proletariat, question. It gave rise to a just social reaction, solidarity among industrial workers in depersonalised plants where machine tends to dominate man. It was important from the point of view of social ethics in reaction against the degradation of man and against the exploitation in wages, working conditions and social security. [*Laborem Exercens* 8]

It must be frankly recognised that the reaction against the system of injustice and harm that cried to heaven for vengeance was justified from the point of view of social morality. This state of affairs was favoured by the liberal socio-political system which, in accordance with its economist premises, did not pay attention to the rights of the workers on the grounds that human work is solely an instrument of production. [*Laborem Exercens* 8]

Worker solidarity is still needed today

On the world level the development of civilisation has revealed forms of injustice more extensive than those which in the last century stimulated unity between workers. This is true in countries which have completed a certain process of industrial revolution. It is also true in countries where the main working milieu continues to be agriculture or other similar occupations. [*Laborem Exercens* 8]

There is the need for ever new movements of solidarity of the workers and with the workers. This solidarity must be present whenever it is called for by the social degrading of the subject of work by the exploitation of workers. The Church is fully committed to this cause so that she can be truly the Church of the poor. [*Laborem Exercens* 8]

Employers – direct and indirect – and the right and duty to work

Work is an obligation, a duty; it is also a source of rights on the part of the worker. Man must work because the creator has commanded it, and because his own humanity requires work. He must also work out of regard for others, his family and the whole human family.
[*Laborem Exercens* 16]

The obligations of justice that bind the worker include fulfilling faithfully and completely whatever contract of employment he has justly and freely made; to do no damage to the property nor harm the person of his employers, and refrain from the use of force in defence of his own interests and from inciting civil discord. [*Rerum Novarum* 17]

The direct employer is the one with whom the worker enters directly into the work contract in accordance with definite conditions. The indirect employer exercises a determining influence on the shaping of the work contract. He substantially determines one or other of the facets of the labour relationship, conditioning the conduct of the direct employer. [*Laborem Exercens* 16, 17]

When we consider the rights of the workers, we must first of all direct our attention to employment for all who are capable of it. The role of the indirect employer is to act against unemployment. In the final analysis this overall concern weighs upon the state; it cannot mean centralisation by the public authorities, but a just and rational co-ordination of public and private initiative. [*Laborem Exercens* 18]

The need for adequate wages, benefits and conditions of work

There is no more important way of securing a just relationship between the worker and the employer than that constituted by remuneration for work, the wage. Wages are still a means by which the vast majority have access to those goods intended for common use; a just wage is the concrete means of verifying the justice of the whole socio-economic system. [*Laborem Exercens* 19]

There must be social re-evaluation of the mother's role and with the need that children have of care, love and affection. Society must make it possible for a mother, without penalising her as compared with other women, to devote herself to her children in accordance with their needs and age. [*Laborem Exercens* 19]

Besides wages, health care, rest and vacations, insurance for old age pensions and injuries at work also determine relations with the employer as do working environment and manufacturing processes that are not harmful. [*Laborem Exercens* 19]

The right to trade union membership, to obtain justice constructively

Modern unions grew from the struggle by workers, especially the industrial workers, to protect their rights. Experience teaches that they are an indispensable element of social life. Representatives of every profession can use them to ensure their rights. [*Laborem Exercens* 20]

Unions are not a reflection of the class structure of society. They struggle for social justice, for a good which corresponds to the needs and merits of working people; if in controversial questions the struggle means opposition to others, it aims at social justice, not to eliminate the opponent. [*Laborem Exercens* 20]

Work unites people. Its social power is a power to build community. Those who work and those who manage, or own, the means of production must be united in it. Labour and capital are necessary to the process of production in any social system. People unite to secure their rights, but their union is a constructive factor of solidarity and it is impossible to ignore it. [*Laborem Exercens* 20]

Efforts to secure the rights of workers cannot be turned into class egoism; with a view to the common good of the whole of society, unions should aim at correcting everything defective in the system.
[*Laborem Exercens* 20]

Union activity enters the field of politics – the prudent care for the common good. However, unions are not political parties struggling for power, and should not be subjected to the decisions of political parties or have too close links with them. Their specific role is to secure the just rights of the workers within the framework of the common good.
[*Laborem Exercens* 20]

We must keep in mind that which concerns the specific dignity of the subject of the work. The activity of union organisations includes efforts to instruct and educate workers and foster self-education. Thanks to the work of the unions, workers will not only have more but *be* more, realising their humanity in every respect. [*Laborem Exercens* 20]

The just rights of members to strike as a kind of ultimatum is recognised as legitimate in the proper conditions and within just limits. It remains an extreme measure. It must not be abused, e.g. for political purposes. Essential community services must be ensured, if necessary by legislation. Paralysis of socio-economic life is against the common good. [*Laborem Exercens* 20]

The worker must in some way be working for himself

The means of production cannot be possessed against labour. The only legitimate title to their possession is that they should serve labour. In general terms, the person who works desires not only remuneration, but to know he is working for himself. [*Laborem Exercens* 14, 15]

The position of rigid capitalism continues to remain unacceptable, namely the position that defends the exclusive right to private ownership of the means of production as an untouchable dogma of economic life. [*Laborem Exercens* 14]

Proposals put forward by the Magisterium take on special significance here: joint ownership of the means of work, sharing by the workers in the management and/or profits of the business, shareholding by labour, etc. [*Laborem Exercens* 14]

Only when, on the basis of his work, each person is fully entitled to consider himself a part-owner of the great workbench at which he is working with everyone else is rigid capitalism defeated.
[*Laborem Exercens* 14]

Agricultural workers

All that has been said thus far on the dignity of work, on the objective and subjective dimensions of human work, can be directly applied to the question of agricultural work. [*Laborem Exercens* 21]

Agricultural work involves considerable difficulties, including unremitting and sometimes exhausting effort and lack of appreciation on the part of society. Added to this are the lack of adequate professional training and objectively unjust situations. [*Laborem Exercens* 21]

In many situations radical and urgent changes are needed. It is necessary to promote the dignity of agricultural work in which man subdues the earth he has received as a gift from God and affirms his dominion in the visible world. [*Laborem Exercens* 21]

Work for the disabled

The disabled person is one of us and participates fully in the same humanity that we possess. It would be radically unworthy of man and a denial of our common humanity to admit to work only those who are fully functional. [*Laborem Exercens* 22]

Careful attention must be devoted to the physical and psychological working conditions of disabled people – as for all workers – to their just remuneration, to the possibility of their promotion and to the elimination of various obstacles. [*Laborem Exercens* 22]

The migrant's right to work

Man has a right to leave his native land for various motives – and also the right to return – in order to seek better conditions of life in another country. This fact is not without difficulties of various kinds. [*Laborem Exercens* 23]

Every possible effort should be made to ensure that it may bring benefit to the emigrant's personal family and social life, both for the country he goes to and the country which he leaves. Much depends on just legislation with regard to the rights of workers.   [*Laborem Exercens* 23]

The most important thing is that the person working away from his native land, whether as a permanent emigrant or a seasonal worker, should not be placed at a disadvantage in comparison with the other workers in the matter of working rights.   [*Laborem Exercens* 23]

8. The international community and economy

It is commonplace today to recognise one international community of nations, however sundered it may be by historical, racial, cultural and economic divisions which challenge its unity. The United Nations Organisation (UNO) set up in 1945 has been a much more widely supported international agency than the old League of Nations. It was an earnest attempt of the democratic countries which had led the war against fascism (1939–1945) to see that the lessons of the past would be learned. They have not quite succeeded, as those divisions testify. Yet much has been achieved, and though the divisions are always threatening to shatter a fragile unity, they have not yet done so. There is also massive support for it from the governments and peoples of the world, who are now more aware of the need for international co-operation because of the modern ease of international travel and communications, and the realisation that all have much more to gain than to lose by doing what they can to maintain the UNO. National independence and the principle of subsidiarity are basic to the international order, as all know and recognise; what is new is that the reality of one international community is now also recognised, and the will to strengthen it – while not yet firm enough – is growing.

The fact that nations are ever more closely bound together by economic ties is one vital source of this new awareness; the problems inherent in the relationship between the so-called first, second and third worlds necessitate a global perspective. The first world is that of the rich industrialised countries of North America and Europe, Australasia and South Africa, with Japan, the oil-rich countries of the Middle East, Africa and South America, and the 'tiger' economies of the Far East. The second world is that of the less prosperous industrialised or industrialising countries of the former Soviet Empire. The third world consists of the less developed nations mainly of the South – Latin America, Africa and Asia. The third world became economically and strategically important during the Cold War of the 1950s–1970s, and therefore politically important too. Forms of economic aid and development were offered to them, mainly out of self-interest, though it was gradually being realised that there was a moral obligation in this respect also. Then, in the 1980s and 1990s, came the rebirth of capitalism after the Soviet collapse, and an increasing sophistication in the financial markets and other characteristics of the economies of the West, which largely abolished the old concept of the international economy – we started to talk about globalisation, and the 'global village'.

The question of the world's population, resources and environment has become a central concern nationally and internationally since the 1960s. The first of these, the population question, is particularly connected with the name of Thomas Malthus [1766–1834]. Malthus, and those of his school, argued that there are physical limits to economic growth, in this case the growth of food supplies. He advanced the famous proposition that population increased in geometric proportion, and productivity in arithmetical proportion – though he gave no evidence for this theory, and it has consistently been shown to be wrong. Had he been right, the human race would have soon reached the limits of subsistence as he had predicted, and thereafter vice and misery would have kept population growth in check.

But the picture was by no means as grim as all that. For example, in the period 1960–1990, when the modern panic about population growth was at its height, although the population of the developing countries increased by two billion persons, world food production exceeded the rise in population by about 20%. Far from leading to increasing misery, 'never before have so many people seen such significant improvement in their lives. Life expectancy in the South rose from 46 years to 62, the adult literacy rate rose from 43 to 60%. Under-five mortality was halved, primary health care was extended to 61% of the population and safe drinking water to 55%' [*Human Development Report* cited in note 6, below].

These figures do not encourage complacency; the last two, about primary health care and safe drinking water, show the great extent of deprivation. In the 1990s, there were still more than a billion people living in absolute poverty, nearly 900 million adults were illiterate, 100 million people were homeless, 800 million went hungry every day. But the overall picture, while it does not allow us to be complacent, will keep away the temptation of thinking that mankind is incapable of doing anything to improve matters; it shows that something can be done if the effort is made.

Furthermore, the truth of the matter is that the concept of the physical limits to growth, which Malthus assumed to be self-evident, is, as one expert put it at the end of the second millennium, 'a faulty concept', because 'if we take into account the creative potential of man, there is no foreseeable limitation to the basic natural resources of food production, which are space, water, climatic conditions, solar energy, and man-made inputs. All these resources are either unlimited or can be expanded, better utilised or redesigned to a great extent. This might be why several experts have denied any upper limits to growth'.[6]

This statement by Wolfgang Lutz is not intended to justify complacency, nor does it do so. While we are, in theory, far from the physical or biological limits to growth, the needs of humanity will be met only if mankind employs the maximum technological creativity, social responsibility, economic initiative and political vision, which are needed to restructure inefficient systems. Every country needs a population policy, some to check decline, others to control growth, according to the different circumstances – but the means must always be worthy of human dignity and not contrary to it.

Connected with the concern about population is that regarding the excesses of the processes of economic development, which have put future resources at risk and endangered the health and well-being of human society, through pollution of the earth and its atmosphere. There is no need to repeat the mistakes of the past if sufficient forethought and resources are put into countering the dangers. When concern began to show on these matters in the USA in the 1960s, one prominent scientist in the field, Laurent Hodges [*Environmental Pollution*, New York 1973] pointed out that if Americans wanted to tackle the problem effectively, all that needed sacrificing was one year's growth in increasing standards of living.

The world has grown even more complex since then, and new problems press upon us. There is always, however, the danger of the over-dramatisation of certain issues by some environmentalists. For example, while most scientists would agree that global warming is taking place, there is disagreement about what exactly it signifies and how much trust can be placed in computer-based simulations of the process. The answer to all the problems that present themselves, as with those of providing for an increased world population, lies in *political will*. Within a democracy we all have a duty to do what we can as free men and women to support those working to this end.

International interdependence

Recent progress in science and technology is a spur to men all over the world to extend their collaboration and association with one another, in these days when the exchange of goods and ideas, and travel from country to another have greatly increased. There is also a growing economic interdependence between states. Finally, the social progress, order, security and peace of every country are necessarily linked with those of every other country. [*Pacem in Terris* 130]

At the present time when close ties of dependence between individuals and peoples all over the world are developing, the universal common good has to be pursued in an appropriate way and more effectively achieved. International and regional organisations deserve the gratitude of the human race. These represent the first efforts at laying the foundations on an international level for the community of all men to work towards the solutions of the serious problems of our times. [*Gaudium et Spes* 84]

The relations between the developed and less developed nations

Probably the most difficult problem today concerns the relationship between political communities that are economically advanced and those in the process of development. Solidarity makes it impossible for wealthy nations to look with indifference on the poverty of other nations unable to enjoy elementary rights. All must co-operate to move goods, capital and men from one country to another. [*Mater et Magistra* 157, 155]

Emergency aid will not go far enough. The only permanent remedy is to provide the scientific, technical, and professional training that the citizens need and put at their disposal the necessary capital for speeding up their economic development with the help of modern methods. [*Mater et Magistra* 163]

Efforts are being made to help the developing nations financially and technologically. All will be in vain if nullified by unstable trade relations between rich and poor nations. When the nations involved are most unequal, market prices that are *freely* agreed upon can turn out to be most unfair. [*Populorum Progressio* 56–58]

Developing nations should not forget that progress has its roots and its strengths before all else in the work and talent of their citizens. Progress is based not only on foreign aid, but on the native resources and their own talents and traditions. [*Gaudium et Spes* 71]

Wealthy nations must give aid and rectify trade relations. The progress of some is not to be sought at the expense of others. Yet nations are the architects of their own development. Donors could ask for assurances, since there is no question of backing parasites and idlers. [*Populorum Progressio* 44, 77, 54]

If, in the years since Pope Paul's encyclical, there has been little development, the reasons are not only economic. The political will has

been insufficient. A world divided into blocks sustained by rigid ideologies can only be subject to the structures of sin, rooted in personal sin – the concrete acts of individuals who introduce these structures, consolidate them and make them difficult to remove.
[*Sollicitudo Rei Socialis* 35, 36]

Christians will have to raise their voice on behalf of all the poor of the world, proposing the jubilee as an appropriate time, among other things, to reduce substantially, if not cancel outright, the international debt which seriously threatens the future of many nations.
[*Tertio Millennio Adveniente* 51]

Population, resources and the environment

Truth to tell, we do not seem to be faced with any imminent world problem arising from the disproportion between the increase of population and the supply of food. Arguments to this effect are based on such unreliable and controversial data that they can only be of very uncertain validity. [*Mater et Magistra* 188]

The resources implanted in nature are well nigh inexhaustible, and man has the intelligence to discover ways and means of exploiting these resources for his own advantage and livelihood. The real solution lies in a renewed scientific and technical effort on man's part to deepen and extend his dominion over nature. The progress of science and technology that has already been achieved opens up almost limitless horizons in this field. [*Mater et Magistra* 189]

Man is suddenly becoming aware that by an ill considered exploitation of nature he risks destroying it and becoming in his turn the victim of this degradation. Not only is the material environment becoming a permanent menace – pollution and refuse, new illnesses and absolute destructive capacity – but the human framework is no longer under man's control, thus creating an environment for tomorrow which may well be intolerable. This is a wide-ranging social problem which concerns the human family. The Christian must take on responsibility, together with the rest of men, for a destiny now shared by all.
[*Octogesima Adveniens* 21]

Conclusion

The social teaching of the Church is an essential part of her teaching on the life of man; Christians are to be fully involved in human society, and guided by the principles of the Gospel in the moral choices that they have to make as social beings. However, these principles are general. How do we apply them in particular?

First of all, the responsibilities of the clergy and the laity in this respect are different. Members of the Church's hierarchy do not have any direct authority over secular society: the role of popes, bishops and priests is to guide the laity through the moral problems involved in social living, not to play an active part themselves in solving them. This is the task of the laity, who find their way to holiness through direct involvement in worldly matters. While it is true that, in some weak or unstable societies at times throughout her history, the Church has become directly involved in secular affairs, on account of the very strength of her social organisation, and the governmental skills possessed by her senior clergy, this involvement did not benefit the Church, but ultimately corrupted her. It is for this very reason that she is wary today of any direct involvement of her clerics in the power structures of the secular world. There are some rare instances where it might temporarily be allowed under Canon law, but these are few and subject to strict control. The clergy are entitled to their political opinions as private citizens, but they must not be politically partisan in exercising their office. By contrast the laity can and – according to capacity and opportunity – *must* be so involved. Just as they are free to choose to marry or not to marry, to follow a trade or profession and to form associations with others, so too are they free openly to support a political party of the right, left or centre.

The Catholic citizen involved in his society must regard the traditions of his country and of the social group to which he belongs as part of a valuable inheritance, even though they will have imperfections since they are a *human* inheritance. Christians must show loyalty to them in general, by patriotism and loyalty to friends, colleagues and associates. They should use the guidance of the social teaching of the Church to try to serve society better, and also as a point of reference, to make them aware of the moral defects in particular aspects of the secular traditions, so that they may seek to counter them by legitimate means.

Catholic citizens must stress to themselves and to others the reasonableness of the Christian view. However, it very rarely helps in secular matters to declare that the Catholic Church teaches such-and-such on a particular subject – it is far better to present the ethical point at issue, and then demonstrate that it recommends itself by its rationality without mentioning its source (unless this is helpful to the argument). If the Church is to have a positive influence on secular society, then we must all have a grasp of at least the basic principles of such matters; such an awareness can then be applied to our own responsibilities within society, in the particular roles that we play.

Our responsibilities to civic society and how to meet them

Civic society embraces the local community and all the private associations in which we participate. There is an overlap here with political and economic society: these private associations can include political parties, business organisations, and trade unions. Here let us just note that the basic obligation to show solidarity with others – which is the key to our responsibility within civic society – is also the key to our obligations in political and economic organisations. In its turn, that very responsibility to show solidarity stems from our basic belief that all human beings, of whatever, race, creed or social background, are made in the image and likeness of God. We should love and respect them accordingly and seek to co-operate with them in any way we can in the pursuit of common purposes. We should never give countenance to anything which encourages one human being to despise another simply because of the accidents of birth. The objective law of God defends the family, the rights of the unborn, the young, the poor, the weak and the aged, and we must do all that lies in our power to see that this law is respected.

The Church's social teaching demands, then, that on the local level, in the local community and its social organisations, we should be good neighbours, active in the local community, and seek the good of each and the good of all. We should be active against injustice in all its forms, and should support local charities and community projects, and work to help the poor and deprived. In other words, we should be good citizens in solidarity with other citizens, and work together for the common good.

Our responsibilities to political society and how to meet them

We are all citizens of a particular state and subject to its government, which has the power to make laws for the common good, and to enforce them under the law. We have a duty to be good citizens and good patriots, and to choose the political allegiance from our own political culture which seems best for securing the common good and defending human rights.

With regard to political authority in general, we must remember that all legitimately constituted government comes from God, and that authority is legitimate when it has been accepted by the citizens, either in a democratic election or, where cultural conditions do not allow there to be democratic procedures, by the readiness of the citizens to live as peaceful subjects of the existing political authority. In such states Christians should do what they can to see that human rights are respected.

We should therefore respect the authority of the state and those in government, while at the same time using what democratic procedures exist to defend our human rights and work for the common good. All Christian citizens of a democracy must participate in its political life, at least to the extent of voting responsibly in national and local elections; those who have the talent and opportunity should be more actively involved through the party of their choice. Where democracy is defective, Christians must try to correct the defects in a constructive way, with a concentration on human rights and the peaceful pursuit of justice. The responsibility of the individual nation state for the well-being of other nations and for a peaceful international order should be borne in mind, and those policies which seem most likely to bring about greater international co-operation should be supported.

Our responsibilities to economic society and how to meet them

Economic society must be based on responsible freedom if it is to do its job of meeting the material needs of the people in a manner which respects the human needs of those who work within it. Individuals must have the freedom to choose what work they do, and the freedom to own productive goods and work them for profit. The state also has the right to own productive goods when the common good requires it. Christians in commerce and industry hold positions as wage earners or salaried staffs, as managers or directors, as shareholders or owners; others hold positions in the professions, the arts, education or the media. Each must try to work with his peers, and in solidarity with them, in trade unions, in trade associations and in boardrooms; but he must also keep an eye on what is lacking from the Christian perspective within each group, and see what can be done to make up that lack, through a striving for the common good, and by the example of hard work and generous self-sacrifice.

While the needs of the consumer are best met through the operation of the markets, nonetheless the market of itself can work for good or ill. The State, which has care of the common good, must see to it that the market respects that good by creating just laws to regulate it. Christians must defend these values. Only those who have the necessary financial resources can bring their needs to the market; yet all should have the means to secure the income that they need through the work that they do. The unemployed and the sick should be supported by the state with the intention of enabling those who can work to do so. A social assistance state should not be created.

Since labour comes before capital, both logically, historically and theologically, it has priority; made in God's image and likeness, the man who works, the subject, is of more value than the object made by it. But labour and capital are not in opposition to one another; they *need* one another. Workers have a right and a duty to work; but they must be aware that their rights stem from a Christian understanding of the dignity of labour. They must testify to this by their personal integrity, by being exemplary workers, as well as through the defence of their rights in association with others. They have a right to adequate economic rewards in return for their work. Employers in their turn have a right to make a profit; however, the common good or the human needs of employees must never be sacrificed in the pursuit of profits, though profit itself is a good since it indicates that resources have been properly used. Workers must in some way be working for themselves, and schemes which allow them participation in management, ownership or profits should be encouraged. They have a right to free association in trade unions, and to struggle for justice where necessary, but they must do so in a spirit of positive commitment to justice, and not one of class war. The state has a right to ensure that public services are available to all even when strikes are justified. Christian employers and wage earners must also model their behaviour on these principles.

International economic relations must be marked by charity and justice. Justice requires that economic relations between developed and less developed nations be based on trade that is fair as well as free. Economic aid should be available to less developed nations when necessary, but it must be borne in mind that each nation is ultimately responsible for its own development, and corrupt politicians and officials must be prevented from diverting aid into their own pockets. Christians as citizens must also do what they can to ensure that their rulers follow policies which will protect the natural environment from destructive forms of economic development. They should support those men, parties and policies which are dedicated to these ends.

'Let us now praise famous men' – and imitate them

This brief survey of the guidance that the Church's social teaching offers should encourage us to commit ourselves fully to striving for the common good. It has shown us that the teaching is not a party political programme; it gives guidance to all social, political and economic groups, and encourages us to work with our fellow citizens of all faiths and none, through the political party of our choice, and through the structures provided for us within our own social, political or economic grouping, to bring justice to all on the basis of solidarity in Christ. We will use this teaching best by absorbing it and applying it, through self-sacrificing example, in the generous service of others.

By following these principles, Christian men and women have changed the world for the good. Let us cite two examples from the twentieth century. Firstly: in the devastation of Europe that followed the second World War, a group of Catholic activists and statesmen, Don Sturzo and Alcide de Gasperi from Italy, Robert Schuman from France, and Konrad Adenauer from Germany, representing the Christian democratic movement in Europe in its various forms, were able to guide the political and economic destinies of Europe into a truly democratic pattern. This did much to heal the terrible wounds inflicted on Europe and the world by the totalitarian democratic tradition which had stemmed from the excesses of the French revolution and its consequences. Christian personalism – which encourages social responsibility in civic society, the family and the community in general, and solidarity and subsidiarity in political and economic society – were their guiding principles, and they worked.

Secondly, in the dramatic events leading up to the collapse of real socialism in the late 1980s, Catholic Poland led the way. Civic society reasserted itself and showed itself more powerful than corrupt political structures. Socially responsible individuals joined together, in the trade union *Solidarity* and in other ways, to outflank and outwit state tyranny. Inspired by Pope John Paul II, who insisted on patience and peaceful methods, *Solidarity* began to challenge the state on human rights issues, and eventually gained such a moral superiority by its methods that the State machine crumbled, leaving the Poles to control their own destiny once more.

These great achievements were the result of commitment to a social cause under the guidance of the principles of Catholic social teaching; the men and women involved in them had absorbed those principles into their commitment to charity and justice, according to the circumstances of their times. In this way we can see that they served the *common* good and not simply their own interests, and worked in solidarity with other such groups to bring about social change. Success in the social apostolate can only come to those who are prepared to discipline themselves so as to live their lives in accordance with eternal and unchanging moral principles; such a discipline produces a generous spirit of self-sacrifice which enables people to win the love and trust of those with whom they are working for the good of society. It is this approach and no other that will enable Christians to confront the many social problems of the age we live in, and of the ages yet to come; to confront them and to win.

Further Reading

The serious literature in English on the social teaching of the Church is limited. The two volumes of my *Christian Social Witness and Teaching: the Catholic Tradition from Genesis to Centesimus Annus* [Leominster 1998] provide the subject with a proper methodology and syllabus. The first volume, *From Biblical Times to the late Nineteenth Century* traces the development of the teaching, taking into account the historical contexts of the development, both sacral and secular. The second volume, *The Modern Social Teaching: Contexts: Summaries: Analysis*, examines some 34 of the documents since 1878 against their historical background, and provides an analysis of each of them. The approach throughout is to try to see what the teaching Church understands its social teaching to be. The footnotes throughout contain brief bibliographies.

More generally:

J-Y Calvez and J Perrin, *The Church and Social Justice*, London 1964. Though dated, this is still valuable.

R L Camp, *The Papal Ideology of Social Reform*, Leiden 1969. This is better than its title suggests, indeed in many ways it was the best attempt in its time at a serious analysis of the teaching in English.

R Charles with D Maclaren, *The Social Teaching of Vatican II*, Oxford and San Francisco 1982. Among other things this provides a useful treatment of the relationship between law and conscience in the Catholic Tradition, as the basis of personal and social ethics.

D Dorr, *Option for the Poor*, Dublin 1993. Counterpoint to Novak's book noted below, it sees the social teaching of the Church through the eyes of a moderate liberation theology, which it hints is superior to that teaching. But it nevertheless takes the latter seriously.

J Gremillion, *Gospel of Peace and Justice*, New York 1975. This represents a creditable attempt to present the social teaching to the post-Vatican II Church, which in the aftermath of the Council did not seem inclined to give it serious notice.

J Hoffner, *Fundamentals of Christian Sociology*, Cork 1963. Has stood the test of time, being republished in 1983 and 1997. The only thing wrong with it is its title. There is no such thing as 'Christian sociology', nor indeed a Christian economics or politics. There is a Catholic *social teaching* which gives guidance on morality in these areas.

J Messner, *Social Ethics: Natural Law in the Western World*, London 1964. Provides a rich source of information on natural law theory and its application to society: indispensable.

M Novak, *The Catholic Ethic and the Spirit of Capitalism*, London 1993. Published in the wake of the collapse of real socialism, many of the aspects of its presentation of the Catholic tradition can be questioned. However that may be, it demonstrates the vitality of that tradition and the debate it occasioned has been fruitful.

M J Schuck, *That They Be One: The Social Teaching of the Papal Encyclicals 1740-1989*, Washington DC 1991. Based on Carlen's great work, it also presents the pre-Leonine corpus. Analysis is in places contentious and pretentious, though overall it is a valuable volume.

Endnotes

1 Man was born for freedom, yet mass slavery existed down to modern times and was accepted by society as a whole, including the Christian community and the teaching Church. This causes problems for the modern mind which is convinced that slavery was abolished by law in the last century in the West, and that this could have been done before if people had turned their minds to it. This is a major over-simplification. Firstly, in the ancient classical world into which the Church was born, it was unthinkable that civilisation could be sustained without slave labour. Even those who saw the evil of it had no prescription for abolishing it; it just was not and could not be on the agenda, and to fail to accept this is to show a total lack of understanding of historical reality. Secondly, white slavery faded away in Western Europe in the central middle ages because social and economic conditions and the Church's influence made it redundant. Black slavery flourished in Europe's colonies and the USA up to the nineteenth century and it was *not* abolished in that century primarily by the anti-slavery movement and legislation: in the early 1840s there were twice as many black slaves crossing the Atlantic, mainly in American ships, as in the time of Wilberforce and Clarkson. It was the Civil War in America, and the resultant emancipation of slaves, which finally spelled the doom of mass black slavery. See *Christian Social Witness*, Vol 1, pp 25, 49, 67, 77, 126, 223, 261, 270, and 315ff.

2 'The Frankish Empire, papal supremacy, monastic foundations and ecclesiastical organisation were the principal springs of medieval civilisation' [C W Previte Orton, *The Shorter Cambridge Medieval History*, Cambridge 1966, Vol 1, p 296]. The Franks were the most able soldiers and statesmen among the invaders, and their need for moral approbation of their rule, and the need of the Church and the Papacy for a protector, led to an alliance between them out of which medieval civilisation sprang – the monasteries and the dioceses throughout Europe being the civilising and law-abiding agents that framed that civilisation. The Church was responsible for all education – spiritual, moral and intellectual – and all social welfare work. The result was that the history of the Church in the middle ages 'is also the history of European society through eight hundred

years when the outlines of our institutions and habits of thought were drawn'. [R W Southern, *Western Society and the Church in the Middle Ages*, Harmondsworth 1972, p 1]. Medieval society 'elected to let the Church lead it'. [J H Mundy, *Europe in the High Middle Ages*, London 1973, p 25]. The 'flowering of new ways of life which grew up around the cathedrals and the universities, royal courts and commercial cities' implanted 'forms of thought and action we take for granted' [George Holmes, *Oxford History of Medieval Europe*, Oxford 1992, page v]. The Church's influence was then generally positive, though it had its down side – in the Inquisition for example. It was over-involved in secular affairs because it was so useful to society in this role – this has a lesson for us today. Such over-involvement detracted too much from her real task. See *Christian Social Witness*, Vol 1, pp 101ff, 133ff, 136ff, 151ff, 170ff, 177ff.

[3] After 1150 Europe moved beyond self-sufficiency in food and could support industrial expansion as the towns attracted the skilled crafts and monopolised industrial production: 'This was the great leap forward, the first in the series that created European Society and launched it on its successful career. It marked Europe's true renaissance two or three hundred years before the traditional renaissance of the fifteenth century'. There is only one event remotely comparable to this, namely 'the creation by the first European settlers in America of the many transit towns linked to each other by road and the other requirements of commerce, command and defence'. [F Braudel, *Civilisation and Capitalism*, London 1984, Vol 3, p 94]. See *Christian Social Witness*, Vol 1, pp 147ff, 195ff, 203ff.

[4] It was the combination of England's economic expansion at home and abroad after the 'Glorious Revolution' of 1688, plus the Deistic influence on some of the enlightenment writers on economics, which paved the way for liberal capitalism. Of the former, Christopher Dawson says, 'Never was the influence of class interests and selfish greed more nakedly revealed in political action' [*The Gods of Revolution*, London 1972, p 17]. Old Whig and Tory interests allied with the bankers and the businessmen, and the bourgeois transformed English society into their own image. Some of the physiocratic early economists transferred the Deistic harmony of the heavens to human society, and persuaded themselves and others that removing all restraint on profit making would usher in a perfect society [E Heimann, *History of Economic Doctrines*, New York 1964, p 49]. It did not. It produced in the first century of the Industrial Revolution the

gross injustices that stoked Marx's fires. See *Christian Social Witness and Teaching*, Vol 1, pp 286ff, 322ff, 328ff.

[5] Marx's response to the defects of liberal capitalism which had made profit the sole criterion in economic affairs, was to elaborate a theory which he said would make the self-destruction of capitalism inevitable – historically necessary – and that the proletariat would rise up to be the agent of that destruction. His great learning in many fields and the moral outrage he showed at the inhumanities of liberal capitalism are impressive, but his was a cure worse than the disease. It 'enabled the Communist party to seize power and exercise unprincipled tyranny in the name of a new metaphysical sovereign' – history itself. [E Kamenka, *Ethical Foundations of Marxism*, London 1971, p 198]. *See Christian Social Witness*, Vol 1, pp 322ff, Vol 2 pp 83ff, 92ff, 266ff, 340ff.

[6] There is a brief general discussion of population and resources in the second volume of *Christian Social Witness and Teaching*, pp 148ff. The figures on population growth, human development and food production 1960 to 1990, are taken from *The Human Development Report 1990*, United Nations Development Programme, Oxford 1990, p 2. Wolfgang Lutz's *The Future Population of the World: What Can We Assume Today?* [London 1996] can fairly well be claimed to be the most authoritative assessment of its subject. Lutz is the leader of the Population Project at the International Institute for Applied Systems Analysis [IIASA], in Laxenburg, Austria, and lectures at the University of Vienna. The IIASA was founded in 1972 and was one of the first to systematically study global issues of environment, technology and development. The statement concerning the concept of the limits to growth is on page 225. On page 197 there is a useful table which examines the predictions about the earth's carrying capacity by recognised authorities over the past one hundred years. They range from 0.9 to 2.8 billion, to 1 trillion and 'no meaningful limitation'.

Index

About the Author

Fr Rodger Charles SJ is Lecturer and Tutor in Moral and Pastoral Theology at Campion Hall, Oxford. He entered the Society of Jesus in 1953 after national service and work experience in the building industry, and was ordained in 1964. His studies for the priesthood included reading politics and economics, and following his ordination he took a doctorate in industrial sociology at Oxford. Since 1968 he has been teaching, researching and writing on the social teaching of the Church, in London, Oxford and San Francisco. His major work is *Christian Social Witness and Teaching: The Catholic Tradition from Genesis to Centesimus Annus*, comprising *From Biblical Times to the Late Nineteenth Century* (Volume 1; pp xvii, 472) and *The Modern Social Teaching: Contexts: Summaries: Analysis* (Volume 2; pp xvii, 493), which was published by Gracewing, Leominster in 1998.

These two volumes were written to provide a methodology and syllabus for the academic study of the social teaching of the Church, and the British Province of the Society of Jesus is funding him in a two-year enquiry into the feasibility of establishing a one-year postgraduate MA, or its equivalent, in the subject, so that those who wish to teach it, or use it in their studies or their work, may be properly equipped so to do. A corresponding society, the *Centesimus Annus Society* (CENTAS), has been set up to facilitate education, research and publications in the field, and in particular to conduct the feasibility study in question; Fr Charles is its secretary.